When You Recognize That Any Change is Filled with *Opportunity* and *Potential*

YOU CAN EXCEL IN TIMES OF CHANGE!

Wouldn't you like to feel confident that you can manage new directions, circumstances, and relationships—that you can take charge of every change, survive it, and use it to expand and enrich your life? Now Shad Helmstetter reveals the seven types of change almost everyone will face, sooner or later in life. He explains the nature of change, and how even changes that will be beneficial in the long run can cause stress, insecurity and anxiety when we have no strategy for coping with them. He then provides six simple, practical steps for dealing with change—your *personal workshop for change.* You'll discover how to anticipate the best and get it; use your personal creativity and find solutions; and make changes happen *for* you. You will have a strategy to follow through any upheaval—a strategy that gives you a clear perspective and resolute inner calm. With Shad Helmstetter's reassuring guidance, you'll develop the skills you need to use any change to your advantage—a program for success that will last you a lifetime!

"WITHOUT CHANGE WE ARE NOTHING.
WITH CHANGE WE HAVE THE CHANCE
TO BE EVERYTHING THAT WE COULD
DREAM OF BEING. . . ."
—Shad Helmstetter

Books by Shad Helmstetter

What to Say When You Talk to Yourself
The Self-Talk Solution
Predictive Parenting: What to Say When You Talk to Your Kids
Choices
Finding the Fountain of Youth Inside Yourself
You Can Excel in Times of Change

Published by POCKET BOOKS

YOU CAN
EXCEL
IN TIMES OF
CHANGE

Shad Helmstetter

POCKET BOOKS

New York   London   Toronto   Sydney   Tokyo   Singapore

POCKET BOOKS, a division of Simon & Schuster Inc.
1230 Avenue of the Americas, New York, NY 10020

ISBN: 0-671-74889-0

First Pocket Books paperback printing December 1992

10 9 8 7 6 5 4 3 2 1

POCKET and colophon are registered trademarks of
Simon & Schuster Inc.

Cover design by Andrew M. Newman

Printed in the U.S.A.

This book is dedicated with admiration and respect, to three of the 20th century's most dedicated pioneers of change: Robert A. Heinlein, Arthur C. Clarke, and Isaac Asimov. Through their works they encouraged me to ask the questions and find the answers, and they inspired me to write about what I discovered.

Since they first influenced my thoughts, Heinlein has passed on; Asimov and Clarke are still with us. Wherever they may be, I trust they are satisfied with the results. They gave us more than they could ever have known.

Acknowledgments

I have been told that few readers seriously read the acknowledgments that are written in the front of the book. It is enough to know that those who are mentioned will read them. This is for them.

I would like to thank my concept editor, Bonnie E. Thomas, for arranging volumes of thought and making my style of writing a sensible alternative to college textbooks. I would also like to thank my editors at Pocket Books, Denise Silvestro and Olga Vezeris, for their understanding, insight, and patience, and their ability to get things right. They are exceptional.

I would like to thank the fine people at Kohl's Ranch in the pine-covered mountains of Arizona, for creating an environment that offered both solitude and inspiration; William Wallace for his constant flow of good ideas and his continued friendship; Debie Friedman for her clarity and perspective; and Don and Rochelle Fann for their unquestioned belief and support.

I would also like to give special thanks to my sons, Anthony and Gregory Helmstetter, who have not only given me constant encouragement, but who have proved again and again that if you want to excel, you can.

For more information on Self-Talk Seminar Programs, or to receive a free Special Information Cassette on Self-Talk, write to The Self-Talk Institute, Dept. F, P.O. Box 5165, Scottsdale, AZ 85261, or call 1-800-624-5846.

Contents

PART ONE

Understanding the Basics of Change

1 Learning How to Deal with Change   *3*

2 Living in a Time of Change   *10*

3 Getting a Clear Perspective on Change   *18*

4 Where Did All This Change Come From?   *27*

PART TWO

The Seven Major Changes

5 The Arrival of Change   *45*

6 Dealing with a Personal Loss   *52*

7 Getting Through the Change of Separation   *60*

8 Relocation—When It's Time to Make a Move   68

9 A Change in Your Relationship   76

10 A Change in Your Personal Direction   92

11 A Change in Your Health   104

12 Personal Growth—A Change in *You*   111

PART THREE

Developing a Strategy

13 The Questions of Change   125

14 The Six Key Steps for Dealing with Change   145

Step 1—Recognize and Understand the Change   146

15 Step 2—Accept or Reject the Change   149

16 Step 3—Choose Your Attitude   152

17 Step 4—Choose Your Style   156

18 Step 5—Choose Your Action   170

19 Step 6—Review, Evaluate, and Adjust   175

PART FOUR

The Change in You

20 Changing Your Perception About Change   183

21 Breaking Away from Average   189

22 Arming Yourself with Stronger Self-Esteem   195

23 Metamorphosis—Getting Ready to Make It Work   207

PART FIVE

How to Excel in a Time of Change

24 Putting the Process into Practice   217

25 The Ten Most Important Words of Change   223

26 Your Personal Book of Changes   240

27 The Ultimate Objective   253

Understanding the Basics of Change

PART ONE

Understanding
the Basics of
Change

1

Learning How to Deal with Change

When we went to school, few of us took a course in dealing with change. It was almost as though our parents and teachers assumed that either we would never have to deal with changes in our lives, or that we would somehow naturally learn everything we would need to know about the subject.

That's unfortunate, because not only is change inevitable, but it sometimes requires all the skill and knowledge we have just to deal with change effectively. And we *don't* somehow naturally learn everything we need to know about change. Dealing with change *should* be taught in school, but because it isn't, most of us grow up struggling with some very tough changes, doing our best to get by—and, we hope, learning from the experience. Then along comes another change. It catches us off guard, and from the way we handle it, you would think we had never had a moment's practice

3

dealing with change. It's as though when the next major change happens in our lives, we have to learn how to deal with it all over again.

It's not because we're not gaining experience. It's because we're taught very little about the *nature* of change—what change is really all about, how to understand it, and how to determine what to do next. In fact, we often don't even recognize true change for being what it really is. Instead, we've given change a lot of "labels."

Divorce, as just one example, is a word that defines an experience that has its underlying roots (and its underlying problems) in what divorce really means: divorce means *change*.

When we're faced with the quandary of whether or not to take the new position at work, we do our best to think it through and figure out what it will mean to take the new job. In reality, the words "new job" or "new position" are just descriptions of another kind of *change*.

When you take up a new interest—let's say playing tennis—and you suddenly devote a lot of time to learning the game, you will likely tell your friends that you are "taking up tennis." That's true; you are. But even something as simple as taking up tennis is also a description of something else—it is a description of *change*.

Change has a thousand names and a thousand descriptions. Everything new that will ever happen to us is another definition of that same basic concept— change. So it is surprising that we spend less time in school learning how to deal with the *basics of change*—than we spend learning to play tennis or starting a new job or getting a divorce! It is as though our parents and teachers taught us everything they knew about "*things*," but they didn't teach us all that much about what makes "things" work.

Telling a young person "You'll just have to learn for yourself" or "That's just the way life is—you'll just have to learn to get used to it" is *not* the best way to teach someone how to *excel* at life!

▪ | *What Have We Really Learned About Dealing with Change?*

The principal attempts at teaching people about change during the past twenty or thirty years have come from self-help trainers who have written books and conducted seminars on the "dynamics" of change.

Another arena in which change has been taught has been the classrooms of military strategists, where change is seen as a tool of tactics and logistics. An even more common classroom for teaching about change is in the field of business management. There, as with the military strategists, change is seen as an opportunity, and knowledge of change—especially forthcoming change—is essential to winning battles in the marketplace.

Personal change is also talked about in psychology classes and studied by therapists and counselors; the people in those professions need to know everything they possibly can about how and why people change. But unless we are self-help-seminar enthusiasts, strategists, marketing executives, or therapists, most of us have not spent any time at all learning about the basics of change.

I know people who are forty or fifty years old who have not spent one day of their lives learning—*really learning*—about change. Is it any wonder, then, that stress and the effects of stress in our lives is one of the biggest contributors to both emotional and physical illness in our country today? Why do we have all the stress? Because we have failed to make the connection between change and stress; because we have failed to learn even the most rudimentary fact of one of the most important subjects we could ever be taught.

It is simply a fact that there is a direct relationship between changes in our lives and the level of stress we experience: *Change causes stress.* When our security is threatened, or when we don't know what's coming next, we respond by feeling anxious or by worrying. This anxiety is what causes stress. The change itself, no matter how safe or manageable it might actually prove to be, can start a chain of psychological and physiological reactions—all of which lead to the condition we call stress. Change brings with it a whole host of unknowns. And even though we may benefit from the change, we are first forced to deal with the *effects* of the change—and then with the stress that the change creates.

And stress isn't the only culprit of which we are the victims. What is at the root of insecurity? *Change.* What is always found close to any problem of deep anxiety? *Change*—or something that *should* change but *isn't* changing. What is one of the basics of human life that all people . *want* most, *fear* most, and *need* most? *Change.* What is the only absolutely certain human condition that will exist from the moment of birth throughout an entire lifetime to the moment of death? *Change.*

So it *is* unfortunate that we were taught so little about change. As is the case with so many of the most important values and teachings of our lives, learning about change has been left up to two of the most difficult teachers we have: *experience* and *chance*. And even though we may have gained some experience, it is time to take the results of changes in our lives out of the hands of chance.

■ | A "Personal Workshop" on Change

If in place of reading this book you were to attend a three- or four-day intensive workshop on dealing with change, and it was a good workshop, you would probably come away from the experience: a) knowing a great deal about change; b) having some practical strategies to help you work on specific changes in your own life; and c) knowing more about yourself.

There can be some real benefits to attending an instructional program of that nature. First, you are spending time in the classroom, not only with your instructor, but also with other people who share some of the same problems and goals that you have. Second, you are given personal exercises that help you understand and practice what you are learning. Third, you get answers to your questions so that you can apply what you are learning to specific changes that are important to you in your own personal life. Fourth, a good workshop can be enjoyable and fun, and because of the experience it can stay with you for a long time. Last, and most important, is that a good program of learning usually creates results—which is why you attended the workshop in the first place.

During the past few years I have spent a lot of time conducting workshops such as those and watching the results. But I have always felt that even the best seminars reach only a handful of those who would like to fix the same problems—or reach the same goals—in their own lives. So I have distilled the best ideas and exercises I have discovered and put them between the covers of this book so that anyone can use them, for any personal reason, at any time—and still achieve the same objectives as the in-person workshop.

This book is your Personal Workshop for Change, for you to use at your own time, at your own pace, and to reach your own objectives and results. If a good workshop that you attend in person takes three or four days to take you through the process, you could do the same with this book. Or you could take three or four weeks, or any amount of time that you choose. The "workshop in a book" gives you some significant advantages.

One advantage is that instead of sitting in a room, taking notes and trying to apply the ideas to something in your head while you're sitting there, you can now apply any idea you discover to your real, everyday life. Instead of trying to think—while you are at the seminar—of something in your life that fits the seminar exercises, you can use the personal exercises that are included with many of the chapters in this book at *any* time in your life that you are going through change. That means that you can get some *real* practice trying the ideas for yourself in a way that is meaningful to you.

In other ways, reading this book has some similarities to sitting in a study group. In this book you will find the same "process" that you would experience if we were spending time together at a workshop. We will be covering the *basics of change;* we will focus on where change comes from, why it is different today from what it used to be, and what effects the continuing changes in society could cause in our lives—so you can reach a conscious awareness of how and why the changes around you may be affecting the changes that you're dealing with personally.

We will also be taking a look at the lives and the changes that other people experience, and through their stories better understand what works in our own lives—and what *doesn't* work. We will learn to identify the real "bringers" or "messengers" of change; we'll look closely at them so that we'll know what they look like when they come calling on us. We'll make sure that the key questions about change are answered, and get you started answering other questions for yourself.

We will learn and practice specific steps and strategies that you can start using right away. We'll complete a *personal action plan* so you will know what you want to accomplish, and so you will have the tools you need to help you get there.

In the writing of this book, along with my work in motivational behavior and current research in the field of mind/brain function, I have also drawn on the experience of many years of conducting in-person workshops on self-programming, personal motivation, and making personal choices that lead to setting new directions and overcoming poorly programmed attitudes of self-defeat and low self-esteem.

During that time, and in the writing of five previous books on these and related subjects, I have been confronted time and time again with an exceptionally important facet of personal achievement: At the heart of the frustrations and unfulfilled personal goals of so many individuals is the significant role that change itself—and *the inability to deal with change in an effective way*—plays in their lives.

There *are* ways to deal with changes in a better way, and in this "personal workshop" on change we are going to explore some of the methods that work best.

2

Living in a Time of Change

In order to learn how to excel with the changes in our own personal lives, we're going to first take a look at the nature of change itself, and find out what's happening with change in the world around us.

That change is coming, there is no doubt! It is upon us. These days, it seems as though everything around us is changing. And there is no part of our lives that is not impacted by it. Family, marriage, relationships, work, career, communications, education, politics, religion, personal life-styles—*every part of our lives* is affected by the change that is going on around us.

■ *Now Even* Change *Is Changing*

Today, things are different from what they used to be—now even *change* itself is changing. Something new is taking place; something is clearly happening to change—and what is happening will, in the next few years, affect us more than most of us might imagine.

What was solid and secure just a few years ago is not so solid and secure anymore. What we could count on then we're not so sure of now. A list of life-changing happenings and events in medicine, science, and life-style that have taken place in just the last five years could fill this entire book.

The changes in our world are taking place at an ever-accelerating rate. The confusion, the disorientation, the anxiety, and even the fear that rapid change in our world brings (whether we recognize it or not), makes it more and more difficult to handle changes in our personal lives that we once could have dealt with far more naturally and easily. And it is clear that the acceleration of change is going to continue to go faster and faster.

I have written this book for all of us who are living in that time of rapid, unstoppable, almost overwhelming change, and especially for those of us who would like to excel in that time. If you are reading this book to deal with something that is happening in your life right now, and you're looking for some practical answers that can help you deal with the change, I encourage you to read on. I believe that what you're looking for is here.

If you are reading this book because you are interested in seeing your world and your life and the changes in it from the broadest perspective, then what we will discover together you, too, should find as fascinating and as enlightening as I have.

If you are reading this book as one who is curious enough to wonder what is coming next and where we all fit within those coming changes, then I suspect you will not be disappointed.

How to recognize what lies ahead; how to predict accurately what will likely change in our own lives; how to live with the change and deal with it without fear; how to deal with the changes in our daily lives—in our marriages and relationships, our families, our jobs and careers, our problems and the opportunities in front of us—all of these are important parts of a book about change and how to excel when that change is upon us.

As we begin our process of learning about change and how to deal with it more successfully, I have some recommendations:

1. Following several of the chapters, I have included personal exercises for you to complete or practice. I suggest that you read through or complete each of these exercises. Treat them as you would if you were actually attending a workshop and completing the exercises as a required part of the program. If you do not have the time to write out your answers, then, at a minimum, think them through and answer them in your mind.

2. Set a personal goal to complete this book in a specific period of time. Long or short, you will get the best results if you make this self-monitored workshop a personal project.

3. Consider going through this book—particularly the exercises—with your spouse, mate, or with some other close personal friend. Certain exercises suggest

that you discuss or practice them with another person. Choose someone you like and trust, and go through the exercises together.

I hope you will enjoy the process we are about to go through together. I know you will enjoy the results.

▪ The Objectives You Want to Achieve

The first step in learning to handle change successfully is to understand that *people who are good at dealing with change have learned to simplify the process.* This is especially important now, since change is more complex—and happening at a faster rate—than ever before. This book is designed to give you the tools you need to make dealing with change a practical and workable process.

By the end of this book you will have a strategy that you can follow and implement whenever you are faced with change of any kind. The first step in building that strategy is to help you recognize where you are starting from, and the objectives you want to achieve. To help you get started, complete the following exercises.

■

■ **PERSONAL EXERCISES:** ■
1. How You Dealt with Changes in the Past

Take some extra time to complete this exercise. Review the examples by yourself, or to make the exercise even more effective, discuss the examples with your mate or a close friend.

In the past, whether you were aware of it or not at the time, every change you have gone through has been a process that (a) you handled well or felt in control of, (b) you handled adequately or felt somewhat in control of, or (c) you handled poorly or felt you had no control over. As you complete the following examples, bring to mind specific changes that have happened to you, and rate yourself on how well you feel you have dealt with each of those changes in the past.

For each example, rate yourself as follows:
P = poorly (little or no control)
A = adequately (some control)
W = well (high control)
N/A = not applicable (did not encounter the change)

How You Dealt with Changes in the Past

---

1. *Leaving home*	P-☐	A-☐	W-☐	N/A-☐
2. *Suffering the loss of a loved one*	P-☐	A-☐	W-☐	N/A-☐
3. *Changing jobs*	P-☐	A-☐	W-☐	N/A-☐
4. *Gaining or losing weight*	P-☐	A-☐	W-☐	N/A-☐
5. *A breakup in a relationship*	P-☐	A-☐	W-☐	N/A-☐

6. Entering a new relationship   P-☐   A-☐   W-☐   N/A-☐
7. Moving to a new city   P-☐   A-☐   W-☐   N/A-☐
8. Having children   P-☐   A-☐   W-☐   N/A-☐
9. Getting laid off or fired   P-☐   A-☐   W-☐   N/A-☐
10. An increase in stress in your life   P-☐   A-☐   W-☐   N/A-☐
11. Having someone leave you   P-☐   A-☐   W-☐   N/A-☐
12. Getting a promotion   P-☐   A-☐   W-☐   N/A-☐
13. Taking on a major new responsibility   P-☐   A-☐   W-☐   N/A-☐
14. Getting married   P-☐   A-☐   W-☐   N/A-☐
15. Getting divorced   P-☐   A-☐   W-☐   N/A-☐
16. Ending or changing a destructive relationship   P-☐   A-☐   W-☐   N/A-☐
17. Starting a new career   P-☐   A-☐   W-☐   N/A-☐
18. Graduating   P-☐   A-☐   W-☐   N/A-☐
19. Learning an important new ability or skill   P-☐   A-☐   W-☐   N/A-☐
20. Starting a business   P-☐   A-☐   W-☐   N/A-☐
21. Being sick or in the hospital   P-☐   A-☐   W-☐   N/A-☐
22. Having to deal with drugs or alcohol   P-☐   A-☐   W-☐   N/A-☐
23. Going to work instead of staying home   P-☐   A-☐   W-☐   N/A-☐
24. Staying home instead of going to work   P-☐   A-☐   W-☐   N/A-☐
25. An unexpected financial setback   P-☐   A-☐   W-☐   N/A-☐
26. Having the kids leave home   P-☐   A-☐   W-☐   N/A-☐
27. Going back to school as an adult   P-☐   A-☐   W-☐   N/A-☐
28. Living with war or the fear of war   P-☐   A-☐   W-☐   N/A-☐

29. A change in faith or religion   P-☐   A-☐   W-☐   N/A-☐

30. A change in the membership   P-☐   A-☐   W-☐   N/A-☐
of your family or household

31. Losing something of great im-   P-☐   A-☐   W-☐   N/A-☐
portance to you

32. An unexpected calamity or ca-   P-☐   A-☐   W-☐   N/A-☐
tastrophe

33. A change in the health of   P-☐   A-☐   W-☐   N/A-☐
someone close to you

34. Achieving an important goal   P-☐   A-☐   W-☐   N/A-☐

35. Setting an important new goal   P-☐   A-☐   W-☐   N/A-☐

2. Your Pattern of Dealing with Change

a. To determine your personal pattern of dealing with change, and to get a clear picture of where you stand now, go back to the first exercise and add up your responses in each of the first three categories. Enter the totals below:

    (1) Poorly _____

    (2) Adequately _____

    (3) Well _____

b. Which category of dealing with change did you use most often in the past? (Enter the category with the highest number of responses.)

_____

c. Which category or pattern of dealing with change would you like to put yourself in most often in the future?

_____

3. Your Objectives

By looking back at any of the examples of change you marked "adequately" or "poorly," you should begin to get a general idea of the types of changes you have had the most difficulty dealing with in the past. In this exercise, select at least one—and up to four—specific areas of change that you wish to work on or deal with more successfully. To do this, complete the following sentence:

Specific changes that I want to deal with in the most effective possible way are:

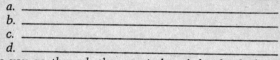

a. _____

b. _____

c. _____

d. _____

As you go through the remainder of this book, keep your own objectives in mind. You should now have some idea which changes in your life have given you the most trouble in the past—and that's the best place to start building your personal strategy for dealing with those and similar changes in the future.

3

Getting a Clear Perspective on Change

It is clear that what happens in our individual lives will continue to be affected by *what happens around us*. Understanding the major changes taking place in our society will help put things in perspective—and having a clear perspective on what's really happening around us helps us manage changes in our own personal lives more successfully.

So before we go through the process of dealing with the individual changes in our lives, we will begin by taking a look at the past to find out where we've been. We will also turn our focus to the present and to the nearly overwhelming changes that have taken place in our own time. We will then take a brief look through the doorway into the future to see if we can get an idea of what to expect next.

Our first objective is to discover how each of us can best deal with the massive changes that are happening *around* us so that we can do an even better job of managing the changes in our *personal* lives. This is a personal program on how you can succeed as an individual in spite of changes—or because of them.

▪ A Look at the Way Things Changed in the Past

Throughout recorded history there has never been any global event to equal what is taking place right now. It is a change in mankind's picture of itself of phenomenal proportions. In order to see this time of change in its real perspective, we have to stand back— quite a ways back—to get even a sense of what is really happening. And to get the clearest picture of what is happening around us now, we have to start by looking at the way in which change took place in the past. We are about to see Earth move from its past to its present in a vast, sweeping panorama of time.

▪ A Few Brief Glimpses of the Past

Our first stop is for a closer look at a time several thousand years before history was first recorded. This is a picture of earliest man, the starting point from which we will measure the progress of change:

A small tribal family from a band of nomads lies in silence inside a cluster of trees at the edge of a clearing, watching as the giant tiger lifts its head, reaching for the scent of fear in the wind, and then turns slowly, its curiosity aroused, to gaze at the trees and the cane where the nomads lie.

The giant beast, with its long, sharp tusks, moves first one step and then another toward the trees—and then, silently and with perfect motion and velvet grace, it is moving fast, low to the ground, charging its prey.

The beast is so strong, so fast, and so silent! The only thing the family crouching at the edge of the trees can hear is the wind in the leaves and the beating of their own hearts. The animal is a master of predators, and mankind clearly has little control over his life or the world in which he lives.

We now move forward in time. Hundreds and then thousands of years are passing by, but there has been little progress. There are only a few scattered families and tribes, and survival is what seems to make up most of the lives these early earth dwellers are living.

Later, after more time has rushed past, we notice that mankind has made a step forward as we stop to observe a singular event in the story of mankind's progress—the discovery of fire. There is a small fire at the center of a camp and over the fire a small boar is being roasted for food. The people that live there now have huts.

So much time has passed that we might have expected a little more to have changed. But not much has changed. What people wear on their bodies is only for protection from cold; they gather food but store little of it; they are frightened by the lightning and the thunder, and they seem to be awed and intensely curious about the bright, full moon moving slowly and silently across the night sky.

The moon that they see never responds to their shouting or to the howls of the animals—and it seems to be just out of reach of the broken bones and the rocks that are thrown at it. The moon, it seems to these distant ancestors of ours, will never be touched by anyone.

In time, a larger village or two begins to form, and then after a thousand years more have passed, the villages grow larger and finally become cities. The early city is more than just a settlement. There are mud streets with oxcarts on them, and where huts once stood there are now buildings of stone and mortar and brick. There are glass windows, wagons and carts, harvested crops and grains, and even storefront shops. Our next stop is even more rewarding. Only a few centuries have passed since the first cities came into being—but now it is not the cities themselves that are important, but what runs and lights them: *Mankind has discovered electricity.*

At this point we are very nearly up to the present. In our brief examination of the history of the earth, we have seen mankind move from taking its first step—and running from the lightning—to mankind arriving at the very threshold of the 20th century. The changes that we saw take place, what few true changes there actually were, took eons—all of history. In thousands of years mankind moved no further than from hunting meat to growing grain, to making a few inventions and making buildings out of bricks instead of huts out of straw.

But as we are about to discover, the 20th century changed all that forever.

■ *A Time of Incredible Change*

In the 20th century mankind somehow got "bigger" than the planet it was living on. It was as though the earth itself no longer dominated and controlled its inhabitants; instead, for the first time in history, the inhabitants were beginning to overwhelm and dominate—rightly or wrongly—the land and the seas and even the skies of the earth they lived on. What do you suppose an observer from a future time would notice about us, and about the 20th century?

What is really different about this century? What is it that sets it apart from all the other centuries of time that went before it? In order to find out, we will now focus on that brief moment in time called the 20th century.

■ *What Really Happened in the 20th Century?*

I will summarize:

January 1, 1901, marked not only the turn of a century. It marked the first day of the final century in an entire millennium. The path that led to the final days of a thousand years in the lifetime of mankind was about to come to a close. And no one who lived then, not even the most imaginative and futuristic thinkers, could have possibly foretold what would happen next. What happened next was fascinating.

Everything changed!

Up to that time, change happened so slowly that most of our ancestors weren't aware of change at all. They were born, they lived their lives, and they died.

One day in their world was like the next, and the next, and the next. What few changes actually took place went almost unnoticed because they came so *slowly*.

Our grandparents and great-grandparents had a pretty good idea where they'd be living, what they'd be doing, and what would be happening twenty-five or thirty years down the road. There were people who lived just a few generations ago who could grow up, live their entire lives, and one day die, in the *same* house they were *born* in. Good or bad, difficult or easy, there was a predictability about the lives they led. For most of our history, from the distant past to the very near present, things remained somewhat the same.

And then, compared to the history that went before it, things suddenly got out of hand. *Change* leaped out of its box, and it leapt with an unleashed ferocity on the world of the 20th century. Suddenly, where there had been quiet and measured change before, there was now a frenzy of it. When the 20th century arrived, in almost a single moment of time, the whole world changed forever—and where change was once something to be dealt with now and then, it was now about to become an unending way of life.

For the first time *ever*, we could no longer say with any certainty what the next ten years or even the next *one* year would bring. And once started, the new roller coaster of change started rolling faster and faster.

■ *The Beginning of* Real *Change*

In just one brief instant of time in the history of mankind, in the first fifty years of the 20th century, we went to war globally—twice. We installed telephones in the average home. We replaced the horse and buggy with the horseless carriage, and then created steel cocoons called automobiles that would hurtle us down man-made highways at more than a mile a minute. We learned to watch the entire world on a television set in the living room. We created jet airplanes and world-wide flight as a means of traveling at breakneck speed from one place to another. We shattered barriers and made breakthroughs in medicine that increased our life expectancy from fifty or sixty years to seventy years and beyond.

We created an entire new arena of science and technology that would present us with a list of almost unimaginable advances—everything from microwave ovens to air-conditioned automobiles to a new kind of electronic technology called computers—and we ran full stride, nonstop, dreaming and imagining and engineering our way into the middle of the 20th century.

But even the achievements of the *first* half of the 20th century paled in comparison to what was about to happen in the *second* half.

In America, the children who were born after World War II opened their eyes to a different world. They now had the benefits of technology, engineering, medicine, higher education, and more promise in their future than ever before—and they were expected to live up to the promise. *En masse,* the children of the new society rushed forward to live up to the expectation—with no guidelines from experience to tell them how to deal with massive change, or what to do next. It was a time of anxiety—and a time of challenges.

It was as though technology—and mankind along with it—entered into a headlong race against time and inevitability. By the second half of the 20th century, what had been good enough just ten or twenty years earlier was no longer good enough. Basic technology became *high* technology. Electrical engineers began to dream of the possibility that the massive vacuum tube computers that once took up entire floors of research laboratories might one day end up as computers that would sit on the desks of their users—and they then proceeded to make that dream a reality.

The field of aeronautics gave way to early space programs that allowed man not only to finally reach the moon, but walk on it! The race to conquer the unknown reaches of space continued, with everything from space probes to Jupiter to the first manned space station in a fixed geocentric orbit above the earth, to space shuttles that could transport men, satellites, and scientific equipment into space and then return safely to earth to be used for mission after mission.

The world of medicine turned from doctoring to research. Medical breakthroughs—*major* medical breakthroughs—became more than expected; they became a way of life. In the field of high electronics, the vacuum tube gave way to the transistor, the transistor gave way to the integrated circuit, and the integrated circuit gave way to the microchip. It was only a short time before even newer technology reduced the stodgy, slow-motion business computers to high-speed, finger-tip-controlled, laptop devices that would allow anyone to compute, communicate, word process, and publish any idea imaginable.

Telephones became interconnected with individual computer control centers; libraries of information came on-line and allowed anyone at any time to open a window to the world.

Society had come a long way from the time—only a few short years earlier—when Johann Gutenberg inked the hand-carved letters of his first crude printing machine and put words on the pages of the first Gutenberg Bible. The time when knowledge was hidden from the masses passed in less than an eye blink to the time when the masses held the knowledge for themselves.

And there were hundreds more advances that took place that I have not even mentioned. The intent is not to diminish them by omission; our purpose here is simply to recognize that *most of them did not even exist in our imaginations just a few years ago.* And the process of change hasn't slowed down for a moment. Today, even the *acceleration* of change is accelerating at a faster and faster pace.

4

Where Did All This Change Come From?

Where did the expectation of all these changes come from? Why are we running so fast? Why are we doing all this? The answer lies not in the fact that one change creates another, but in the fact that we were set up for the changes.

What caused us to get here was not only the technology of the 20th century. What brought us to this point was not first the advancements and the breakthroughs: What pushed us and life around us to a fever pitch of high-motion activity was *a picture that was painted for us in advance*.

The reason we are confronted with nonstop change is not only that a new millennium is here; the reason we are where we are today is that we were *told* that this is where we would be. We have not arrived here by accident. The world that you and I are living in today has come to us by *design*.

Let us see who created that design.

■ Who or What Is Creating All This Change?

Over the years, as I began to study the effects of the many changes in our lives, I began to look for the cause of the changes. If mankind had lived for so many centuries with a slow and almost measured kind of change, what has caused us to be living with so *much* change now—so little predictability?

Who set all this change in motion? I wondered. Certainly it could not be the result of the invention of modern technology itself. It must be something more than that. Where did the technology itself come from in the first place? Technology does not have a mind of its own. Then what, or who, was the mind behind it?

When I was just entering my teens I was fascinated by many kinds of literature. But the stories of the future were the most intriguing to me. I read stories that were wildly fascinating, beyond possibility, it seemed—stories of space flight and electronic magic that could exist only in someone's imagination—or so I thought at the time. Today, only a few short decades later, those same stories would read as though they came from yesterday's newspapers. There is nothing futuristic about them. *They are not impossible; they have already happened.*

Could it have been the writers who wrote about our future, I wondered, that created our present, and the future in front of us? As I was to learn, for the most part it was. At least that's where it started.

■ *Turning Dreams into Reality*

Throughout recorded history there have been writers of ideas, dreamers who went as far as their imaginations would take them. But before the 20th century the dreams were only dreams, and for the most part nothing could be done with the dreams. There was no way to make the dreams happen.

Such was the case for those who, since man first walked on the earth, had dreamed of flying above it. It is easy to imagine a young boy in earliest times watching a hawk or an eagle soaring in the sky, floating motionless on the wind. That boy, whose family knew little more about life than the hunting of animals in the forest, could have only dreamed of one day flying like the birds in the sky—but there was nothing at all that he could do about his dream.

Even later, when centuries of time had given man logic and measurements and engineering—even then, men like da Vinci, Galileo and Newton could still only dream of man in flight. Leonardo could create intricate drawings of mechanical apparatuses, and even make models that looked as though they should work—but even Leonardo was destined to remain forever exiled from his greatest dream; *he would never fly.* The technology, the knowledge to support the dream and to give it life, had not yet been invented.

And so it was that throughout all of history, until very late in the 19th century, and more completely by the second half of the 20th century, the dreamers could do nothing more than dream. When it came to bringing to life what they imagined, the dreams of men like Jules Verne and H. G. Wells were ultimately reduced to the capability of the tools they had available to them.

The thinkers had learned that it would take more than imagination to create a different world—it would take the right *tools*.

With the arrival of the 20th century, those tools began to be created. And with the new tools, after remaining technologically—and physically—grounded throughout all of history up to that moment, suddenly in another blink of the cosmic eye, everything took off. As the 20th century exploded with unimagined growth in *every* area of human endeavor, the development of the technology that came along with it placed the "dreamers" in a completely new position. *For the first time in history, the availability of new technology surpassed society's ability to use it up!*

All at once mankind had more inventions and more tools than it knew what to do with. Imagine the leap of experience to move from an almost primitive mode of survival and maintenance—to a mode of imagination and attainment! It was the beginning of incredible, unstoppable change. It was the beginning of the future.

■ The Beginning of the Future

It was at that moment in time, sometime during the middle of the 20th century, that we began to realize that it just might be possible to deal with nature and the world around us on our own terms. We might be able to have some control over our environment instead of waiting helplessly by while the environment we lived in—and even our physical bodies, our struggling brains, and the laws of natural physics—hemmed us in and controlled our lives completely.

It was during that moment in time that a few imaginative and yet practical future thinkers like Isaac Asimov, Robert Heinlein, A. E. Van Voght, Ray Bradbury, Arthur C. Clarke, and others sat down at their typewriters (and later, at their word processors) and began to write.

In so doing, it was as though those writers sat together in front of a grand Pandora's box, opened the padlock on its front, pried open the lid, and unleashed their vision of the future on the world.

Suddenly the writers of the new science were not just writing fiction about the future; they were predicting it—*and then creating it!* Never was the theory of self-fulfilling prophecy so powerfully proved. For the first time in history, the dreamers were able to inspire the minds of people who had the tools to create the future. Before that moment, people could only imagine taking flight with the birds or traveling to the moon, but they were completely powerless to do anything about it. And then, suddenly, the dreamers of our generation could dream of going to the moon, and then *go* there!

It was a case of imagination creating the demand for technology which then inspired greater imagination. More imagination led to new ideas, and those ideas led to the demand for new technology—and so on, and so on.

■ *We Saw the Future—and Made It Come True*

If the dreams of the futurists had been principally limited to the words in books, their imaginative stories of life in the future might have affected us in some small way, but I doubt that we would have taken their stories to heart and begun to believe that the picture they painted would actually become a way of life. What convinced us that such future stories could become reality was not just the writers themselves; it was the other dreamers of the 20th century that brought the pictures to life.

Let's look at just one example of how dramatically the self-image of an entire nation can be influenced by a single "minor" event—in this case, a motion picture.

Once Stanley Kubrick and Arthur C. Clarke left us moved and pondering at the end of their futuristic movie, *2001: A Space Odyssey,* manned space exploration—which was not then a reality—would never be the same. Neither would our picture of the future be quite the same again. In one dazzlingly brilliant flight into space, that one single motion picture event took us there. We had been in space. We had felt its weightlessness and heard the quiet of its almost-absolute vacuum.

The movie gave viewers a completely new—and entirely believable—experience. Not only did the "new futurists" show us a picture that was so real that it made us finally believe we could reach outer space; in one incredible motion picture they showed us what the technology would have to look like to get us there. They gave us the picture, and we bought it and ran with it. We believed we could make it *happen*—and an entire generation got ready to head for the moon.

That is an important example of what we're talking about, but it is only one example of many. By the end of the 1980s it was possible to see the future by watching "future movies" that were played on a home TV video player—also something that had not existed just a few years earlier. An imaginative new era in the entertainment industry created hundreds of future-think motion pictures, and of those, dozens of them were spectacular, breathtaking, and ultimately inspiring.

We were literally pushed into the 21st century by imagination and technology—disguised as entertainment. But those vivid, powerful pictures of our future were imprinted in our minds forever. How could we deny our role in creating the future when we had already seen it, touched it, experienced it, and *accepted it as part of our reality?*

Just as the imaginative minds of these visionaries gave us new pictures of our universe, so did they and other futurists also present us with a nonstop flow of ideas and pictures and experiences of what the *rest* of our world would soon look like.

We could not even flip through the channels of our television sets without seeing programs that showed us the future of medicine, education, transportation, communications, architecture, global politics, world economy, sports, leisure time activities, and psychological breakthroughs—all presented as a look at the future, and all of them well on their way toward already becoming a reality.

It is no wonder we became caught up in the exhilarating race to the 21st century. *We had already seen it*—and now it was up to us to create it!

Had there been a grand plan, a universal scheme on the part of some secret political mastermind group, to change the world and push it headlong into the future, they could not have done a better job of it. One by one, the new futurists were influencing and changing our society forever.

From the standpoint of natural, programmed human behavior, we had no choice. We had an unconscious social responsibility to make the 21st century what we had already imagined it to be—what it was supposed to be. And for the most part, what it was supposed to be was a future that was far, far better than the century that went before it.

What the 21st Century Is Supposed to Look Like

According to the more positive futurists, in the 21st century we are supposed to fix the problems with education; we are supposed to win the war on drugs; we are supposed to cure the common cold, cancer, and epidemics of any kind; and we are supposed to make major progress toward halting the effects of aging.

By the 21st century, we are supposed to be able to hurtle from city to city on rails of air or antimagnetism, empty our prisons, solve the problems of crime in the streets, and be raising a new generation of beautiful, healthy children who all go to college and carry encyclopedias of knowledge around with them in their pocket computers (and they will solve the rest of the world's problems that we do not have enough time to deal with).

By the dawn of the next century, we are supposed to begin a new age of peace, health, and prosperity. That is the promise of our new technology. That is the positive picture of the bright new world of the 21st century.

And it is *that* picture that, collectively, as a society, we are even now racing to complete. It isn't that we're talking about it when we go home at night. It's not that we sit around and have boardroom meetings and planning sessions and discuss whether or not we're living up to the responsibility of our collective social unconscious and its race to the future. But we have been *programmed*, both individually and as a society, to seek a destiny that we unconsciously believe to be the best tomorrow that we have been shown.

Each passing year, as the last page on the calendar is turned, we are reminded again that the time to live up to the expectation of our own destiny is already slipping past, and we may be losing ground. The result? We are running at high speed, and there is no end to the race. All we have to do is look around us and observe what is happening. We are living in a world that is caught up in change, and there is nothing—*absolutely nothing*—short of global cataclysm itself, that will stop that change from happening.

If that much *is* happening, if everything around us is changing that fast, if we are in the middle of a race and going faster and faster by the minute, if there is nothing to stop us, what will happen next?

■ A World of Nonstop Change

The past few years alone should give all of us a lesson in overcoming shortsightedness. Think how many things we take for granted today—most of which did not even exist only *twenty or thirty years ago:* satellite weather forecasting; electronic banking; closed-circuit classrooms; modern, over-the-counter miracle drugs; fiber optics; instant photography; color television with stereo sound that picks up sixty-six cable channels at the push of a button; digital music, video disks and video cassette recorders; space shuttles and orbiting laboratories; electronic games; electronic synthesizers and musical instruments; heart, kidney, lung, and liver transplants; laser surgery; birth control pills; in vitro fertilization; modern cosmetic surgery; robotics; communications satellites with instant worldwide telephone and television service; shopping malls; computerized supermarkets; freeze-dried food; fast-food restaurants; microwave cooking; portable cellular telephones; electronic voice mail; home facsimile machines; personal computers and in-home electronic offices; two-income families and day care centers . . . *and the list goes on and on.*

And those changes around us create dramatic and sweeping changes in our personal lives—everything from our relationships and families to where and how we go to work, what we do there and how we do it, where and how we live, how often we move, what our goals are, how successful we are, what we think about, how we spend our time and who we spend it with—literally everything about us is changed by the changes around us.

Even at this moment, the full list includes literally tens of thousands of products, developments, and advancements that influence, affect, and change our lives in tens of thousands of ways. In time, that list of "impossibilities" that will become changes in our everyday realities will be endless!

If in medicine, electronics, technology, neuropsychology, science and engineering, and individual life-style—if in these areas and in many others we have come as far as we have in just a few short years, then we will go even further in the *next* few short years.

The question now is not whether or not new change is coming. It is whether or not we recognize it for what it really means to us *personally*.

■ How Well Will You Deal with Change?

In the brief picture of change that we just saw, we did not focus on the picture of those who were overwhelmed by the change and who lost out because of it. But if we could look clearly, carefully, and accurately at the real picture of the change that is already with us, and if we took the time to examine what we saw, we would also have to see a picture of those who are losing out—*a picture of those who do not know how to use the changes in life to excel*.

If we looked, we would see those who were not prepared, or who could not accept the change as a part of the new, "natural" order of things. And because they could not understand what was happening to them, their lives would be turned upside down, or lessened, because of it.

Change as a way of life is more upon us than some

of us would like to admit. What you and I choose to do about the coming change—or, for that matter, the changes that are already upon us—will determine how successful we are in the years that lie ahead of us.

Will unstoppable change direct and control your life for you, or will you learn to use the changes, take advantage of them, survive in spite of them, and expand your potential because of them?

The increase in high technology alone has added new responsibilities for all of us. It should be obvious to us that living in a time of accelerated change has become a way of life that places more demands and stresses on us than ever before. As you go through the process of defining and gaining control of the changes in your life, you are being asked to perform at a level of activity beyond what even your own parents and grandparents had to deal with. But give yourself a break. You are having to deal with more change in a shorter period of time. Most of us have been doing our best—but there are some things you can do to get ahead of the game.

■ | *Your Personal World of Change*

It is time to turn our focus from the world around us back to our own worlds, our own personal lives, and the changes that go on within them. We have seen that the world is moving rapidly around us, creating greater and greater turbulence—which inevitably affects our private, everyday worlds as well. We also know that there is very little we can do to slow or stop the turmoil of changes "out there." But what we can do is understand the reason for the changes and take the effects of those changes into account when we are dealing with the changes in our personal lives.

We can use the external changes—the advancements or the challenges—in the world around us to help propel us forward. But it will be the manner in which we learn to manage and conquer the changes in our personal lives—in spite of what may be happening around us—that will determine our success in learning to excel.

■

■ PERSONAL EXERCISES ■
Recognizing the Effects That External Changes Have in Your Life

---

1. *In each of the following areas, list three ways in which your life has been affected by the external changes that are currently taking place, or that have taken place during the past five to ten years:*

a. List three ways in which your marriage or personal relationship has been affected (examples: length of relationship, nonnuclear family).

(1) _____
(2) _____
(3) _____

b. List three ways in which your job or the work you do has been affected (examples: work environment, high-tech equipment, more frequent job changes).

(1) _____
(2) _____
(3) _____

c. List three ways in which your income, money, or finances have been affected (examples: instant access to your money, two-income families, higher use of credit).

(1) _____
(2) _____
(3) _____

d. List three ways in which your need to learn new information or skills has been affected (examples: knowledge of global marketplace, becoming computer literate, increased specialization).

(1) _____
(2) _____
(3) _____

e. *List three ways in which the way you communicate with others has been affected (examples: more long-distance calling, facsimile, electronic voice mail).*

    (1) _____
    (2) _____
    (3) _____

f. *List three ways in which the way you spend your spare time has been affected (examples: cable TV and VCR, priority on family, more leisure travel).*

    (1) _____
    (2) _____
    (3) _____

g. *List three ways in which your personal life-style has been affected (examples: faster paced, more conveniences, increased time demands).*

    (1) _____
    (2) _____
    (3) _____

h. *List three ways in which your health and fitness have been affected (examples: the food you eat, diet and exercise programs, total fitness awareness).*

    (1) _____
    (2) _____
    (3) _____

i. *List three ways in which the attitudes, life-styles, and activities of your friends and associates have been affected (examples: friends change more often, busier, less available).*

    (1) _____
    (2) _____
    (3) _____

j. *List three ways in which your stress level or peace of mind has been affected (examples: higher overall stress, less quiet time, more turmoil and confusion).*

    (1) _____

(2) _____

(3) _____

    k. *List three ways in which your personal goals or directions have been affected (examples: accelerated goals, more demands and expectations, greater emphasis on achievement).*

    (1) _____

    (2) _____

    (3) _____

    2. *Check one or more answers. Do you generally see change around you as:*

      a. Moving too fast _____

      b. Confusing or unsettling _____

      c. Moving at just the right pace _____

      d. Creating problems for you _____

      e. An opportunity for you _____

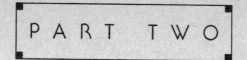

PART TWO

The Seven
Major Changes

5

The Arrival of Change

The kind of change that seems to cause us the most problems is the change that is created outside of us, the kind of change that it seems we have nothing to do with. It happens *to* us or *in spite of* us. This is the kind of change that most easily makes us feel out of control, or makes us feel that the change is in control of our lives instead of us being in control of it.

We're going to look now at the kinds of change that seem to be brought about by the events of life. There are many such changes, of course, but we are going to focus on those that are most important. Of all the kinds of change that appear to *happen* to us, it is these seven major kinds of events, or these seven "messengers" of change that often create the greatest turbulence in our lives.

It may seem odd to refer to major changes as *messengers* of change when it looks like they are nothing more than the changes themselves. But the point is that a major change is major because it is not as simple as it seems. The real impact of these major changes, the real reason they create such problems, is that they announce the arrival of a whole host of other effects in our lives. Thus, the Major Changes, though changes themselves, are also the "bringers" or the "messengers."

The Seven Major Changes are:

Loss
Separation
Relocation
A Change in Relationship
A Change in Direction
A Change in Health
Personal Growth.

Here are some of the things the Seven Major Changes have in common:

1. They are changes that happen to all of us.

Few of us get through very many years of life without being confronted by each of these Seven Major Changes. At some time, each of us experiences *loss;* we lose someone or something that is important to us, or that we hold dear.

In time, each of us experiences the change of *separation*—when we become separated from something or someone we care about, and would rather hold close.

Nowadays, almost all of us experience the change of *relocation* as we move from one home to another, from one city to another city, or even across the country—maybe several times. All of us have seen the effects of changes in our *relationships*.

Even the most stable or unchanging individual experiences what happens when he changes his *direction* and goes a different way. If we live long enough, we will probably undergo one or several changes in *health*—to better health or lesser health. And if we are alive and working at it, we all (we hope) experience *personal growth*.

It is almost as though the more alive we are, the more in touch we are with life, the more often we could experience these Seven Major Changes. They are encounters with living.

2. These changes appear to happen without our control.

Another similarity among these seven Major Changes is that it looks as though they happen independently of our will; it may at least appear as though we have nothing to do with them at all—and that may be true. That's why they make us feel out of control. These changes make up much of what we might call the force of destiny—that fate that befalls us and forces us to alter our course through life no matter how hard we might try to ignore it or fight it off.

We do our best to hold things together in a kind of predictable norm. We try to find security in something, *anything* that we can count on. Sometimes that something isn't even good for us—like a relationship that is hurting us, or a job that we know will not lead to advancement—but we cling to it and hold on to it because in spite of what it may be doing to us, at least it helps us feel that some things remain the same.

But each time one of the Major Changes arrives, we are left once again with the feeling that we are not so much in control of life as life is in control of us. So pervasive is this feeling that in time, with enough of these changes happening to us, it is all too easy to eventually give in and accept as fact the belief that life deals us the cards it holds, and there is nothing you or I can do about it.

There are those who fight that notion, of course. The banner they carry says, "You create your own reality, and nothing that happens happens by chance alone." Yet, it can be difficult to believe that you are the master of your own universe when a loved one has just died, or you have lost your job, or you suddenly become ill, or after thirty years of being together, your marriage falls apart and one of you files for divorce.

Even when the messengers of change bring positive news, and a new adventure is about to enter your life, it can still seem like the new opportunity you are facing is happening *to* you—that the planning of it looks suspiciously more like someone else is writing the lines in your life's script, and you are expected to act out whatever role the writer has scripted for you.

We may choose to write our own scripts, but the Seven Major Changes will go on trying to convince us that we are at best the coauthor, and it is life itself that writes the most important scenes we play.

3. Each of these Major Changes always brings more change with it.

Major changes like *loss, separation, relocation, relationships, direction, health,* and *personal growth* create *other* changes that go far beyond the initial event itself. They seldom just happen and then go away without creating any ripples in the water around them; they usually create waves! These are events that start a whole chain reaction of other events happening, so when we face one of these changes, we're never facing that change by itself; we're also having to face all the changes that come along with it!

The change in a relationship with a mate or spouse, for example, can change a lot more than what happens to the relationship itself. It can change what you do with your evenings, how you spend your time, what you think about, or even what you do with the next years of your life.

A change in direction can very often bring with it a change in location; that, in turn, can bring a change in relationships along with a separation from the security of the past. If things go well, and you deal with the change effectively and excel because of it, the initial change also brings along with it personal growth. If the change in direction, and relocation, and separation were traumatic enough, it could also bring a change in health—and, of course, if the relocation and separation were substantial, the change could even bring about loss.

The messenger of change that appeared to be arriving was a change in direction. Yet that one change brought with it most of the other Major Changes.

So the initial change itself is not what creates all the turmoil—it is the changes that come along with it. No wonder change can be so unsettling! When it comes, it brings its friends! As we examine each of the individual kinds of change, we should look carefully to see what other changes will come in the door when the first change arrives. Unless we are prepared to greet them and know what to do when they arrive, those changes will come in, sit down, make themselves at home, and work their way into the rest of our lives.

4. The greatest problem with these changes often comes *before* they arrive.

As is so often the case in dealing with change, it isn't just the change itself that creates stress and anxiety and other problems. It is the *thought* that the change is coming, and the fear of what it may bring.

So instead of having to deal only with change and its aftermath, we go through a similar kind of trauma just *expecting* it. In that sense, we add to the amount of potentially negative or positive effect that the change can have on us. We experience the results of the change—or we emotionally "experience" the change itself—*before, during,* and *after* the change takes place.

And unfortunately, because anything that's coming brings something unknown, it is easy for us to imagine the worst instead of the best. It is easier to believe that something will go wrong or work against us than it is to believe that same event will automatically work well, create happiness, and make our life better.

Let's say, as an example, that the event itself—this particular messenger of change—is the change of relocation, moving from one place to another. Depending on your level of personal security and your enthusiasm for making the move in the first place, you could choose to dread it and set yourself up to go through more fear and hardship than the move itself will bring, long before you make the move. In this case, it isn't the event of the change taking place; it is the anxiety of dealing with it in advance.

An obvious problem with this is that creating trauma in advance is unhealthy from almost every point of view. Because of the stress and related effects it brings, it is emotionally unhealthy and often physically unhealthy as well to worry about a change before it happens.

That isn't to imply that we naturally fear the Major Changes. What we think about them in advance—how much we look forward to them or fear them—depends on the change we're facing, on our attitude about the change, and on the confidence we have in ourselves.

You don't have to know for sure that the change is coming. In fact, the change itself may never happen. But in expecting it or dreading it, the anxiety can be just as great as if the change had happened and you were already living it.

The point to recognize is that each of the Seven Major Changes carries with it the potential of creating its greatest change even before it arrives, simply by the way in which we set ourselves up for what we think is coming.

When we experience a Major Change, it is easy to think that it is that change itself that is the most important event that is happening at the time. But as we shall see, the change that is the most noticeable— the "event" itself—may not be what is causing the problems or disrupting our lives. It may be something else entirely.

Let's take a look at each of the Seven Major Changes—these messengers of change—that play such a vital role in each of our lives. Is there anything that can be done about them, or is it just up to each of us to accept them? Must they so often be our adversaries— or could they become our strongest allies? Let's find out.

6

Dealing with a Personal Loss

The first Major Change that we will look at is *loss*. This can be the loss of anything that's important. It could be the loss of a job or income; it could be the loss of a hope or a dream; it could be the loss of a keepsake, the loss of a friendship, the loss of a loved one, or even the loss of face or position or self-esteem.

The only parameter is that the sense of loss is great; it is important or profound, and it has more than passing meaning in our lives.

I remember the first time I saw loss, and recognized it for the life-changing event that it was. When I was a boy of nine or ten, a tornado struck in the farm country not too many miles from where my family lived. The tornado struck at 9:20 on a Friday evening in July. Shortly before noon the next day, I went along with my father in the family car to visit the farm where my aunt and uncle, Elda and Otto, lived. My parents had gotten word that the tornado had touched down in that area, and the phone lines were out. My father wanted to make sure everything was all right.

There is no way I could have been prepared for what I saw as our car drove up the long driveway to the farm. Where the barn had been there was nothing but a shredded mass of splintered wooden planks and rolled and twisted sheets of aluminum that had been walls and a roof. The tall wooden poles that had carried the phone lines and electricity to my uncle's home were now nothing more than short stubs of post, torn off just a foot or two above the ground. A wood slat corn crib had shattered itself into matchsticks. I would never again refuse to believe someone who tried to tell me that the wind of a tornado was so violent that it would drive pieces of straw into wooden fence posts; I saw it for myself.

All that remained of the house were the back steps and the front porch. Both of these were completely untouched. But in between them, where the house had been, all that remained was the big concrete hole in the ground that was the basement. Later on, as I tried to describe the scene to my friends at school, they would not believe me when I told them that I had seen the old farm pickup truck lying on its back, wrapped around and around, completely bound up in the wires from the electrical lines. The battery from the old pickup truck was found inside what was left of the refrigerator, lying in a field a quarter of a mile away.

Just two weeks earlier Otto and his family had visited us for Sunday dinner. Otto talked about how he was planning to build more corn cribs near the barn before the end of the summer, before it was time to pick the corn in the fall. He looked very positive and prosperous as he talked about how good the crops were that year, how things had been improving, and how maybe farming wasn't such a bad life after all.

And then, less than two weeks later, on that Friday at 9:20 in the evening, the first Major Change called loss arrived at Otto and Elda's. When it came, it didn't just knock quietly at the door and wait to enter. When loss came calling at my uncle's farm, it took the door and the house and everything else with it. Nothing for my uncle and his family would ever be the same again.

It is not hard to imagine the hardships, the readjustments, and the sense of insecurity that that kind of loss created in their lives. That one change—*loss*—upset their stability, their routine, their goals—almost everything about their lives. And they were completely *unprepared* to deal with it. Instead of taking a short while to assess the situation, adopting an attitude and a style that would pull them through, and implementing a strategy that would help them get on with their lives—they were devastated.

At the time I was struck by how profound their sense of devastation was. But later I was even more aware of how totally their loss was *continuing* to disrupt their lives. I wondered why they didn't put it past them and move on. I could not understand why they would let their loss stop them completely.

It would be much later that I would have an answer to that question. And the answer would lie not in whether or not they had been *prepared* for the change—but whether or not *they knew how to deal with change.*

■ *Another Kind of Loss*

It is fortunate that loss doesn't always have as great an appetite as it did when it arrived at Otto and Elda's. Sometimes when it comes, it is more selective.

A friend of mine named Helen was an executive in the insurance industry. She had been with her company for seventeen years, and had played an important role in creating the company's growth and success. When on occasion we met, my friend Helen was the perfect picture of success. She had worked hard and had weathered corporate storms over the years, and it would have been hard to find an example of someone who was more secure in her life and in her work.

Then one day change came in the form of an announcement that the company had been sold, and new management would be stepping in to take the company over. It was clear that Helen was about to become a casualty of corporate change. Seventeen years of working and building was about to be lost, and with that loss, Helen's life was about to change.

■ *A Loss Can Live Forever*

I was seventeen years old when one day, while working around the house, my mother lost the diamond from her wedding ring. It was a small diamond, but to her it was the most beautiful diamond in the world. I couldn't understand at the time why that evening, after searching our home from one end to the other, over and over again, my mother sat down and cried. "She could get another one," I thought. "All diamonds look pretty much alike."

Even at that age I could feel the pain coming from her, but I couldn't understand what she had lost. Many years later, when we celebrated my parents' golden anniversary, she still mourned that one loss from so long ago. My mother's diamond did not last forever. But the loss of that diamond is with her still.

And then there is what seems to be that greatest kind of loss. When I was two weeks short of my thirteenth birthday, my cousin Douglas got sick. Doug was the best friend I had ever had; he was just two weeks older than I was, and his mother and my mother always said we looked so much alike that Douglas and I could be twins. Douglas came down with what we all thought was the flu. But it got worse, and they decided to take Doug to the hospital for a checkup. It was three days before his birthday.

On Saturday night the family visited him and made plans to come back to the hospital on Sunday morning. Douglas got to choose the kind of birthday cake he wanted, and everyone felt good that he was doing so much better. The next morning Doug's mother baked an angel food cake and frosted it with his favorite whipped cream frosting, and then she and the family left for the hospital with the special cake with thirteen candles on it. But something had gone wrong. Douglas died only a few minutes before his family got there. He never got to eat any of his birthday cake.

I had lost my cousin and my best friend, and it was the first time that I really began to understand what that kind of loss feels like. But it must have been nothing like the terrible and tragic pain that Doug's parents felt from the loss of their son.

■ *The Other Major Changes That Come with Loss*

It is easy to see why loss is such a difficult change to accept. It doesn't come alone—ever! Along with any important loss always comes *separation;* it can often cause a change in a *relationship;* it can bring with it a change in *direction* in life, and if the stress of the loss is too great, it can bring a change for the worse in *health*. And, of course, if understood, dealt with, and risen above, the loss—no matter how difficult it might be at the time—can also bring the positive change of *personal growth*.

Together, these other Major Changes joining up with the original change—the loss itself—can represent a formidable team of changes. The problem is that we usually do not identify the rest of the team members. We think about what we have lost and what that means to us, without recognizing what's really going on—that *other* changes come along with the loss.

That's because when we know it is a group of changes all posing as one, we may be overwhelmed. We get confused. We feel lost or insecure. One change brings on another, and then another, and we suddenly find ourselves dealing with a whole battery of unknowns.

Otto and Elda, as an example, moved, quit farming, changed their vocations, and changed most of their plans for the future. And Helen, the insurance executive who lost her job, moved across the country, changed her career path, and literally started a new life. In her case, because of her attitude and because of the way she dealt with it, she improved her life because of the change.

It's no wonder that for most of us, losing something terribly important makes us feel suddenly alone, at a loss, out of sorts, and unsure. *It isn't only the loss itself that has suddenly entered our lives; it is the other changes that go along with it.*

Once you are aware of that, you have a better chance of dealing with it. Recognizing what you're really dealing with—a whole group of changes at once—may not get rid of the grief or the sorrow or the fear or the anger entirely—but it will help. You know what you're dealing with; you see things more clearly. Things start to make sense again, and the confusion begins to be replaced with understanding, and then with action, and, in time, with healing.

■

■ PERSONAL EXERCISES ■

1. *Name at least three significant losses that you have experienced in the past (or are dealing with now):*

a. _____

b. _____

c. _____

2. *Rate how well you feel you handled each of these changes (poorly, adequately, well):*

a.

b.

c.

3. *List one thing you have gained from each of these experiences:*

a. _____

b. _____

c. _____

7

Getting Through the Change of Separation

Separation is a primary change. It is one of the first kinds of change most of us experience and remember. The kind of separation we think of first and usually remember longest is the separation from someone, usually a close friend or someone we love. But separation is also the change of being apart from anyone or any*thing* that is important to us. The change can come as a separation from your job, from your home, from a group of people you are used to being with or are close to, from school, from a life-style, even from a possession.

Some people immediately think of separation as that period of time just before divorce or reconciliation. But the real definition of the change of separation is simply being apart from something that is important to you.

Some people become separated from something that is important to them, and remain separated from it all of their lives. It either still exists and is out of reach, or it remains only in their minds—but to them it still exists, so instead of seeing it as a loss, they see it as a separation.

Separation differs from the change of loss in that separation is more likely to be temporary. The feeling of separation is also different from the feeling of loss. With loss we have the feeling that something that was ours is now gone; with separation the feeling is more that something that is ours is still there—it still exists as *ours* or as a part of our lives but there is a problem of proximity or availability. What we miss is still there; we just can't gain access to it.

Another important difference between loss and separation is that loss usually implies a negative; separation doesn't have to. Getting away from something, moving on, putting something behind you, or just having a different mental climate can be healthy. So separation itself as a Major Change is not necessarily a bad thing to happen. But whatever its reason for being, separation does bring change, and it is that change that can work even better for us if we are aware that it's there.

The type of separation that plays the biggest role in our lives is the separation that leaves us with a space when it is gone. It is a space that seems to demand that nothing can fill it up except what was there in the first place. It's easy to understand the importance of this change when the example we use has to do with people we are close to. You probably remember well the first time when someone you cared a lot about went away.

It is important to recognize that it is through our understanding of each of these Seven Major Changes that we can learn how to deal with them and how to use them to our benefit and growth. The first step is to learn to recognize them *for what they really are* when they arrive.

■ *Katherine*

Katherine had worked for the Department of Education for thirty-four years. At one time she had been a grade-school teacher in the elementary school in the small town of Madison, where she lived. For the past twelve years Katherine had been District Director of Junior High Curriculum, and in that capacity she spent three or four days a week on the road visiting the various schools in the district, meeting with teachers and department heads, designing new curriculum programs, and measuring the effectiveness of the programs and the students' progress.

At the age of fifty-eight, Katherine planned to spend many more years managing the programs she had developed and was now coordinating. She loved the hours on the road driving to all the other schools and towns that made up her district. Katherine looked forward to the school and the teachers and even the students that she would be meeting and working with that day.

Katherine's husband, Maxwell, had died six years earlier. Max had been the superintendent of the Madison public school system, and he and Katherine had been completely devoted to each other. It had taken two years just to deal with the loss, and then another year for Katherine to find herself again. She had stayed with her job, and that had helped; things had finally gotten back on an even keel.

Now it was a Saturday morning in May. Katherine was expecting a visit from Marvin Jensen, an old friend and a member of the school board. Marvin said he had some school business he wanted to talk over with her, and Katherine was looking forward to his visit. She heard the screen door open and close on the porch, and then a knock at the door. Katherine had no way of knowing that Marvin was bringing with him a message of the arrival of the Major Change called separation; he had come to bring Katherine news of a change that would affect almost everything about her life.

For the next fifteen or twenty minutes Marvin talked, explaining how the school board had met, and in a final vote late last evening had decided to enact a complete consolidation of all the schools in the district. The new school would include the office of the Director of Curriculum—but that position would no longer require outlying school visitations, hours on the road traveling from school to school, meeting with teachers and principals, and visiting classrooms.

This was different from the loss of her husband Maxwell; this was a separation from almost everything that Katherine had learned to trust and rely on—the long drives in the country, the days spent monitoring the progress of school after school, making her way to each of them like a visiting headmistress keeping a watchful eye over her students.

In just thirty days Katherine's old job and her complete way of life would be gone forever. She wasn't losing her job. She still had her career. But now things were about to be so different as to be almost unrecognizable. Katherine was to have an office at the new school with a meeting room attached, and teachers or staff would visit her there, and then they would leave the meeting room and go about their business—and Katherine would sit in her office and look out the window and wonder what had happened to her wonderful life.

As Marvin spoke to Katherine, he first saw the eyes of a bewildered and frightened woman. But then he saw the look begin to change as Katherine realized what was really happening: her friend Marvin had brought a message of *change!* How she dealt with that change would be entirely up to her—and Katherine was not going to let it stop her for a moment. The look that Marvin saw in Katherine's eyes now became the look of a strong-willed, resilient winner—the look of one who overcomes the odds and learns to excel in a time of change.

Few of us ever see the arrival of change in any special way. Change "happens." We react to it, do our best, and hope everything works out all right. That's all most of us ever learned to do. It would help if we could learn to recognize the arrival of change as Katherine saw hers in the message brought by her friend Marvin.

It is when you learn to recognize the arrival of change, and know it for what it *really means*—the arrival of *opportunity, plans,* and *action*—that you gain an entirely different focus. You then have a clearer perspective, and you can begin to put into motion an actual mental strategy for dealing with that change—a strategy that puts *you* in active pursuit of the best plan of action.

Use this method of recognizing each of the Major Changes—like Katherine in the story—and learn to see them for what they really are and what they really mean to you. We'll look at several other examples in the following chapters that will help you get some practice in learning to identify the Major Changes and being able to recognize them when one of them calls on you.

▪ Emotional Separation

There is another kind of separation that does not have to be a *physical* separation—it can be a separation in the *mind*. You've probably known someone who could live in the same house with someone else but still be emotionally separated from that person.

Many parents often go through this with teenagers. The parents begin to lose touch with their kids, and the harder they try to force an understanding between them, the more alienation they create. Then the teenagers become more distant and walled off. They start to trust in their friends more than in their parents. What once would have been family discussions now turn into arguments, or, worse, into sullen silence. The parents demand and the teenagers retreat.

Day by day, brick by brick, the wall between them grows. After a while it is a wall that is too high to see over and too strong to break through; there are no doors or windows in the wall, and you can't reach the other person at all.

That is as much a separation as if the teenagers lived in one city and the parents lived in another— maybe even worse.

The same kind of mental or emotional separation takes place between married people and in other close personal relationships. We have all seen it happen. You can live in the same house but you are miles apart.

So when you are identifying which of the seven major kinds of change you might be dealing with, be sure to recognize *emotional* separation when that is what is happening. This Major Change—*emotional* separation—comes more quietly than *physical* separation. It may not even knock on the door or announce itself at all.

Emotional or mental separation almost never happens in a day or two; it usually takes months, sometimes years. Then, finally, the two people involved may move apart physically. The separation is more apparent—it is physical; it can be identified. And by then it is often too late to do anything about it.

If the Major Change called *emotional separation* were to speak to you, I suspect it would say, "Beware. Be careful. You may not know I'm coming, you may not know I'm here, but watch for me. Look for me. Listen for me, and recognize me *now*, before it is too late." Of all of the Seven Major Changes, this is the only one that may have arrived long before we know it.

When we go through a loss, we know it. When we are apart from someone or something physically by space and distance, we know it. When the messenger of change comes that tells us it is time to move, and we are about to find ourselves in a new home, that message of change is clear to us. When we set a new direction in life, we are conscious of taking that step. When an important change takes place in our health, for better or for worse, there are almost always signs, or we can feel it. And when we experience personal growth, when we improve ourselves and become greater than who we were before, we recognize the change by looking in the mirror and by the way we think and by the way we feel about ourselves inside.

But emotional separation is more subtle. If we fail to recognize its presence, it will find a way to let us know it has arrived. The best time to deal with emotional separation is long before it arrives.

■

■ PERSONAL EXERCISES ■

1. In general, how well do you feel you deal with the separations in your life?
- [ ] *Poorly*
- [ ] *Adequately*
- [ ] *Well*

2. On an average, how would you rate your sense of personal security?
- *a. Generally insecure* _____
- *b. Somewhat insecure* _____
- *c. Somewhat secure* _____
- *d. Highly secure within yourself* _____

3. What is the single most important separation you have experienced?
_____

4. Was the separation your choice, or was it someone else's?
_____

5. Name three things you did that made the time of change work better for you.
_____
_____
_____

6. What would you have done differently to handle the changes created by the separation more successfully?
_____
_____
_____
_____
_____

8

Relocation—When It's Time to Make a Move

Dennis and Carol lived with their three children in a small home in a west Chicago suburb. Dennis was the assistant marketing manager for a small high-technology firm that designed and marketed computer accessories. Carol worked as a registered nurse. Their sons, David and Mikie, were both students, and their daughter, Kimberly, attended preschool.

Dennis had worked very hard to get where he was in his young career. He had gotten his first job in the sales division after only a year and a half of college. But he had gone back to school at night to earn his associate degree and was now well on his way to his bachelor's. Things were going pretty well for Dennis and Carol, but they both hoped to continue to work to make things better.

In spite of the fact that even with two incomes Dennis and Carol had to be careful with their finances and live modestly, and in spite of the fact that they did not yet have a boat or two new cars or some of the other things some of their friends had, what they did have was a feeling of security in their lives. They had the feeling of belonging. For Dennis and Carol, their work and their schedules and their plans, their family and their friends, were things they could count on.

During the past year Dennis had received a few phone calls from possibly interested employers, companies in the same line of business who might be interested in hiring Dennis away from his current job. But Dennis wasn't really expecting anything to come of those calls.

Then one evening, just after he and Carol and the children had finished dinner, the phone rang and it was for him. When Dennis answered the phone, the voice on the other end of the line could just as well have said, "Hello. I'm one of the messengers of change, and I'm about to change your life." The call was about a new job, in another city—and the major change that was about to arrive was the change called *relocation*.

In just two months Dennis and his family would be living in new quarters in a new city, 2,122 miles away in California, where they would be beginning a new life. In less than sixty days they would have uprooted nearly everything that they relied on, everything that Dennis and his family had faith in, and he would ask his family and himself to sacrifice nearly every moment of security that they held dear.

For more than an hour Dennis talked with the man on the other end of the telephone. There were so many things to consider, so many things to think about, so much change, so much uprooting—and all for something that he had worked for and dreamed of achieving. Dennis learned that he would be offered a salary that was nearly twice what he was making now. The company that wanted to hire him was big, and the position itself that was being offered to him was at least two steps above anything Dennis had hoped to reach in the next five years.

Even as this messenger of change spoke to him, Dennis began to think about what this change really meant. Almost nothing would be quite the same ever again. All of the comfortable sameness, the security that was so valuable to Dennis and his family, the quiet and almost simple home life, the Sunday dinners with Carol's grandparents, the scout troops, the campouts in the summer—everything was about to change, and all because of that one word that meant nothing more than "to move"—the word *relocation*

■ *One Little Word Spelled M-o-v-e*

Relocation can be from one home to another 2,122 miles away, or it can be from one part of a building to another. Relocation can be as simple as a change in status and the office that goes along with it, or as uprooting as leaving home for the first time and venturing out into the world. And moving—for whatever reason, whatever distance, and to whatever place—can be exhilarating, trying, fun, traumatic, filled with hope, exasperating, an adventure, heartbreaking, uplifting, dreadful, wonderful, painful, filled with apprehension, filled with opportunities, and, at the least, life-changing.

■ A Relocation of My Own

I will never forget the time when I was twelve years old and in the seventh grade and my family decided to move from the brittle, cold winter in the Midwest to the eternal summer of the Southwest. I had never lived in anything close to a big city before, so from the time the move was announced to us, and even throughout the move itself, I was filled with youthful enthusiasm and a spirit of incredible adventure.

My parents probably saw the whole thing differently, but my brother and sisters and I saw it as a time of unlimited new chances to see the world—or, at least, another part of it. If there was a messenger of change who visited my parents and prepared them for what was to come, he must have given them a different message from the message I got about the change. I thought everything would be great!

Three days after we arrived in the new city, I endured the calamities of finding a new place to live and being enrolled in a school that looked to me to have several thousand students who were all bigger than I was—all of whom seemed to take a special interest in mentally and physically destroying any new student who had arrived from a small town in the Midwest. The town that I came from had a total of just over two thousand inhabitants, and my seventh grade class that I had grown up with had less than eighty students. I was completely unprepared for what was about to happen.

My dreams of newfound adventure and the possibility of experiencing a whole new wonderful world were shattered the day I walked into my first class in the new school. As I pieced it together later, I had three strikes against me right from the start: The first was that I was a naive new kid in what appeared to be a totally hostile and alien environment. The second was that in my limited experience I really believed that most kids were friendly and would like to be your pal.

But the third strike against me was the worst. I wore glasses. At that time, in the wrong school, there was no greater distinguishing characteristic that would brand someone almost irrevocably as the eternal prey for the macho appetites of seventh-grade bullies than the wearing of glasses. The first words that I heard from the low-level taunts and jeers from my more darker-minded classmates were the words "four-eyes" whispered in low, menacing tones that sounded much louder and frightening to me as I walked into the classroom and sat down.

The homeroom teacher, Mr. Frazier, who also taught English first period, seemed to me to be oblivious to the almost instant character assassination that had greeted me when I walked in, as he beamed a smile and introduced me to the class. He could have been announcing the next subject for execution. The words from somewhere in the back of the classroom, "*Let's get him at lunch*," that sounded almost louder than the teacher's introduction, rang alarm bells in my mind. This was not at all like I thought it would be. I didn't even know these kids, but being an individual of sound mind who was capable of intellectual reasoning, I came to the conclusion that I was in trouble—*big* trouble.

I remember sitting at that desk during homeroom and throughout the English class that followed, hardly daring to look around or daring to confront what I might be up against. I could only have wished that sometime before I had arrived and found myself in this obviously life-threatening situation, I would have been visited by a wise and kindly messenger of change who would have told me what to expect and how to deal with it.

But like so many others, I had no idea what to expect. It is a lasting tribute more to my athletic skills as a gymnast and a wrestler than to my ingrained positive attitude about people that I survived somehow and came out of it alive. In time we worked things out, and as the next months went by, I even made friends with some of the kids who had been the toughest and the most difficult to get to know.

Now, many years later, when friends tell me that they are moving to another city to follow their careers or to make a new start somewhere else, and their kids will be enrolling in new schools and are certain to find new opportunities in front of them, I think about the parents, and I think about the kids, and I think about how difficult that can be for all of them. Over the years the messenger of change that announces relocation has visited me many times. In time, I have learned to listen to his message. Moving even a part of our life from one place to another, no matter how close by or how far away that may be, almost always creates more changes in our lives than we had bargained for.

■ Once Again, One Change Leads to Another

As we have already seen, one Major Change tends to bring other changes along with it. Moving from one place to another often brings with it the change of separation or loss, changes in relationships and even changes in direction.

What is especially interesting about this is how often we make a move without *consciously identifying* its results! We of course think about the obvious results of the change—the new job, the details of the move itself, the logical reasons for making the move in the first place, and the expected enhancements that we believe must await us at the end of the journey. But few of us were trained to be strategists in the art of changing.

As a result, a lot of what we do is to go along with what happens next. The issue we think about is the change or the move itself, and the more obvious results of that change. We plan the move, call the moving company, pack up our belongings, get in the car or get on the plane and fly off to the future, never fully recognizing that in taking that one small step, we are about to change our lives for now, and probably our entire futures—forever.

If we ever want to get in control of the situation, and learn to excel through change, it is important for each of us to learn to recognize the impact the change of relocation can have on our lives. The reality of relocation is that making the move from one place to another is as natural to life in our high-speed world as two-career families, going back to school as an adult, or flying halfway across the country for a weekend. There is almost nothing left to keep us home. The nuclear family is almost gone, and with it, the last ties that bound us to home are also gone. That sweeping, upsetting, unsettling, and challenging third messenger of change called *relocation* is a fact of life. So be ready for it. When it comes, you can choose to use it, choose to make the best of it, and choose to excel because of it.

▪

▪ PERSONAL EXERCISES ▪

1. What one word best describes your personal feelings about moving? _____

2. In the most recent important relocation you have made in the past, which of the following most accurately describes your attitudes, actions, and feelings? (Check each response that applies.)

    a. Stressed _____
    b. Generally calm _____
    c. A negative attitude _____
    d. A positive attitude _____
    e. An adventure _____
    f. A bad experience _____
    g. A good experience _____

3. What were the most important factors that made your relocation—for you—a bad experience or a good experience?

    a. _____
    b. _____
    c. _____
    d. _____

4. What could you have done to make the change work better for you?

    a. _____
    b. _____
    c. _____

5. What other significant changes took place in your life because of the move or relocation?

    a. _____
    b. _____
    c. _____
    d. _____
    e. _____

9

A Change in
Your Relationship

An important message of
this book, and the process of looking at change differently, is that the more we know about change, the
more we understand its nature—and the more we are
in control of how we react to that change, the more
successful we will become, not just in dealing with the
changes themselves, but in other important areas of
our lives. The more we understand how completely
and pervasively changes in the world around us are
affecting literally *everything* about us, the more we
increase our chances for coming out on top.

The alternative is to let an entire world of escalat-
ing change batter and buffet us around, upsetting our
lives, undermining any foothold of stability we might
have had, and destroying our security and sense of
well-being so that we constantly stay thrown off guard

and wondering where the next assault of change is coming from.

There may be no better example of this almost overwhelming chaos than in our homes and families. It is astonishing to think that it was only a couple of generations ago that most people got married, raised families and *stayed* married. I'm not questioning the possible moral message that gives us; I am simply pointing out a fact that is a result of a new world of unharnessed and chaotic change.

Nowhere has the explosion of change in our times had a greater effect than in our personal relationships. Two-year or even two-month marriages are common. "No-marriage" marriages are a way of life. Children grow up knowing two or three different sets of parents and grandparents. They don't necessarily like the idea, and life for many of them is a series of shuffles from one home to another, but at least they can take heart in knowing that *they are in the majority* among their classmates. For many people, there is little stability left.

In our fast-changing world, we are dealing with a domino effect in which one change leads to another. But we are not dealing with just one row of dominoes. The entire tabletop is crisscrossed with rows and rows of dominoes, and they all interconnect so that one change leads not to just one other change and then another, but a whole network of lapping and interconnecting changes lead to a complex matrix of changes that has the appearance of causing all of the dominoes to fall at once.

The fourth Major Change, the messenger of change named *relationship*, may be the busiest messenger of all. He certainly has his hands full. It is safe to say that you cannot get through life without being visited by this messenger. The relationship could be between husband and wife, close friends, parents and children, relatives, enemies, lovers, associates at work, bosses and employees, brothers and sisters, classmates, stepchildren and stepparents, doctor and patient, therapist and client, or grandparents and grandchildren.

Any of these relationships can be positive or negative, or any degree in between. What matters is only that it is an important relationship. And a significant change in *any* relationship that is important to you can change your outlook on life, your level of attitude, and the pattern of your actions. When you have a change in an important relationship, the result is that some other areas of your life will change along with it.

I know people who lost their jobs because they went through a difficult divorce. I know others who have isolated themselves from their families for years because of a fight that started way back when with a parent or an adult brother or sister. I have known people who entered a relationship, and, after seeing it fail, changed their feelings almost entirely away from ever creating another strong relationship again. They convinced themselves they couldn't trust anyone and that a deep relationship would never last.

But these repercussions caused by a change in a relationship could have been minimized or avoided completely if the people involved had learned to recognize and deal with the minor signals that indicated a major change was in the making.

Let's look at a list of actual circumstances that often take place in even the best relationships, that are actually minor changes, or *changes in the making*, that you can begin to recognize and deal with for what they really are. The minor changes, or signals, that are included on this list can take place in any important relationship. They could occur in your relationships at home, at work, with friends or relatives, or with anyone who is important to you.

■ | *Dealing with Minor Changes,*
  | *Avoiding Major Problems*

In reviewing this list, you will probably recognize that, in most cases, when you treat these events as actual *changes* and deal with them accordingly, you:

a. Have a far better understanding of what is actually taking place

b. Give yourself the opportunity to follow a specific plan of action

c. Prevent small changes from growing into problems that are much harder to handle, and could eventually threaten the relationship itself.

Here, then, is a list of everyday situations which are actually *changes* themselves, that you can practice dealing with as they come up. And thereby you can do a better job of dealing with changes that occur in your relationships:

- A change in personal goals or direction of one of the partners
- A recurring argument about the same thing
- A recurring dissatisfaction with the relationship
- A change in interest
- Devoting more time to something new
- A change in the requirement for personal "space"
- An increase in complaining by either partner
- A decrease in physical closeness

- An increase in the stress level of either partner
- A significant change in appearance (e.g., weight, style, personal grooming)
- Developing or increasing an unhealthy or unappealing habit
- A sudden increase, decrease, or change in communication
- A change in the showing of courtesy or consideration
- A change in the other partner's acceptance of your thoughts or ideas
- Spending time with a new friend
- A sudden rebellion against rules or authority (especially among children)
- A change in the amount of effort either of you puts into the relationship
- A shift of position or control in the relationship
- The feeling (on your part) of wanting to escape, avoid, or minimize time spent together
- Unusual time or attention devoted to someone or something else
- Medically unsupported signs of illness, depression, or reduction in physical activity or libido
- A change in the use of discretionary income without discussion or agreement
- An apparent, unexplained change in your job, position, or status
- A change in the other person's loyalty to you (siding against you at work, etc.)
- A "coolness" or distance in an important friendship
- Being "left out" or not being included in the same way you were before
- A change in your interest in the other person
- A general change in the other person's disposition

• A change in the words you use—the way you talk to the other person

Whether you are now in a good relationship, in a relationship you feel is in jeopardy, have just lost a relationship you cared about, or are looking for a new relationship, that list of events can let you know in advance that a major change could be on its way. And when the major change named *relationship* arrives, you can be sure that you are about to say hello again to some old friends called emotions.

■ Strong Relationships—Strong Emotions

The reason that changes in relationships can be so totally upsetting to our lives is that the reaction to the change is almost always *emotional. The stronger the relationship, the stronger the emotion.* In fact, it is the emotion itself that makes the relationship strong in the first place. It makes sense, then, that when the relationship changes, it is our emotions that get stirred up.

That is why we "fall" in love. We don't logically and reasonably step into love as a part of a strategic plan that is calculated and laid out in advance. That's not love; that's a business venture. When we fall in love, it is our emotions that take over and guide us (or misguide us), and it is indeed our emotional mind and not our logical mind that is in control.

When you move from making an acquaintance, to "falling in like," to falling in love, the messenger of change called *relationship* would tell you, "Be careful. Go ahead, but get ready: you are about to throw reason out the window and put your life in the hands of an autopilot that is running on almost pure emotion."

■ It's What's Happening in the Brain

I mentioned earlier that few of us, when we were in school, took classes on how to deal with change effectively. It is also true that when we were in school, few of us were taught how the programming processes of the human brain work and why we think and act and feel like we do. In fact, when many of us were in school, those who taught us didn't know enough about how the brain worked to teach it to us.

To simplify an extremely complex biochemical and physiological process in the brain, here in part is what causes our emotions and why they can be so powerful:

Emotion is *chemical*. That is, what we *feel* as emotion is actually caused by the release of minute quantities of very powerful chemicals in the brain. Those chemicals, when released, immediately affect our attitudes, our sense of well-being, and other completely physiological responses. The more of those chemicals that are released in the brain, the stronger "feelings" we have. The release of those chemicals is triggered by thoughts and by our unconscious reactions to a situation.

Let's say that Jackie is sitting at home in the evening relaxing and watching television. She is feeling fine; she is a little tired, but she's in a good mood and feeling comfortable. Then her husband, Les, comes into the room and, right in the middle of Jackie's favorite television show, starts to criticize her for spending money that day on something unnecessary. A long-standing argument rekindles, and in minutes the sparks are ablaze and Jackie's emotions jump to the boiling point.

Let's say that Jackie and Les have had a lot of practice at this same argument, so it doesn't take long for things to get out of hand. The conversation now sounds a lot more like shouting than conversation, and someone listening in on the conversation might think that the two of them don't really like each other that much. That may not be the case, of course, but that is what it sounds like.

If you could see, on a computer screen, a measurement of the effect that one simple, short argument has on Jackie's internal chemical control system, you would see some amazing biochemical changes in the chemistry of her brain.

Neuroscientists have learned that all our thoughts and experiences are recorded or imprinted permanently in the brain—chemically and electrically. The analogy most often used is that the human brain is like a personal computer. Everything you say, hear, see, think, or do is "recorded" or programmed into the brain just as though it were being typed into a computer. We have learned that:

a. Thoughts create emotions.
b. Our emotions are actually biochemical responses in the brain.
c. The brain records thoughts and experiences chemically and electrically, and stores them permanently.
d. Those experiences or mental messages become "programs" in the brain.
e. The stronger the feeling or the stronger the

emotion, the stronger the programs those emotions will create in the brain.

f. The strongest programs in our brain determine what we will do next.

The result is that things we feel strongly about create the strongest computer programs in our brains. And the day-to-day actions we take that directly affect our relationships are based on those strong, feeling-based mental programs.

Huge files of mental programs that determine how we feel about ourselves and how we feel about the other people in our lives get stirred up and shifted around when we suffer a negative change in a relationship. Those same programs and those same mental files also get topsy-turvy when the opposite happens—when we suddenly wake up one morning and realize that we have fallen in love. Just as there are people who disrupt or sabotage their successes because they handle a downturn in a relationship badly, there are also those who seem to come to life with a vibrant new energy when they find themselves stepping into an exciting new relationship, or when an old relationship suddenly blossoms and comes to life.

Think back now to the feelings you had when you first fell in love. What happens to our mental chemicals and our programs in the brain when we fall in love is beyond comparison to almost any other human experience. The thrill, the exhilaration, the fear and the hope that that one experience brings on, puts into play a powerful programming mechanism in the brain, which in turn can literally take control of our judgment, our feelings, and our actions. (That is what makes love blind.)

If emotions such as love, fear, anger, and joy, are

based on chemically exaggerated or "heightened" programs in the brain that are *that* strong, it's no wonder a change in an important relationship can create such a shock to the system. The change that's taking place is actually causing chemical changes in the brain. That change that takes place is playing with your emotions. And those emotions are chemical responses that are based on the most powerful programs that you carry in your mind.

■ Our Programming Affects Our Relationships

The picture of the two people having the argument at home in the evening can be looked at as a picture of two people responding to their own mental programs, releasing strong chemicals into their systems without even knowing it, and allowing the chemical emotions that result to take over the argument for them.

So it is necessary, when we take a look at what happens when a relationship changes, to also look at what *causes* our almost unreasonable reactions and behavior when a relationship is not going well. If we understand the importance of the programming of our own human brain, we can understand a great deal more about why we react the way we do when a relationship goes bad or when love is lost. We also can understand why we react the way we do when love is found, when a friendship works, and when our relationships are going well.

■ When You're Not the Only One Involved

In whatever way we can be affected by any of the other Major Changes, the effects are almost always exaggerated or magnified when the change has to do with a personal relationship. And there is another reason for this beyond the natural emotional chemistry of the brain.

In any of the other changes that we're dealing with, such as loss, separation, new directions, a change in health, or relocation, the change is taking place in those situations almost as an *event*. The change "happens" and you can watch it take place—like watching it on a theater screen in front of you. You are there, you participate in the change, and it affects you, but it can continue to happen without any real interplay between *you* and the *event* itself.

When you are moving from one place to another, as an example, the event of that move is not really a player with human characteristics—the event simply takes place, and you observe its happening, and you are part of it. As another example, when you go through a loss, the loss happens to you or it impacts you—and once the loss has happened, whoever or whatever it is that you have lost is no longer there. When the loss is complete, it is gone.

But a major change in a relationship is different. The relationship can change dramatically, but it still *exists;* it is still there. If the relationship that is changing happens to be with someone you love or care about a lot, and the relationship is beginning to break down or has fallen apart, it is usually not here one day and completely gone the next. The other person can still be there, and that means that along with the strong emotions that *you* bring into the change, you are suddenly dealing with a similar set of strong emotions from the *other* person as well!

So when a major change in a relationship takes place, you are not dealing with just one set of feelings; you are dealing with two sets of feelings—*two complete sets* of emotions and goals and fears and attitudes and everything else that makes up the two people involved.

Your emotions and your thoughts by themselves may be strong enough to create a hard-hitting impact on your life. Now add the other person's feelings and emotions and attitudes and actions to the same brew.

Instead of having one powerful force of change working by itself, you now have two powerful sets of forces and energies at work—yours and the other person's. Put those together like a chemical mixture, add in the emotions, and stir them up with actions and thoughts and every word you say, let them boil for a while, and maybe even turn up the heat, then stand back and watch what happens.

We see the extremes of this kind of change especially clearly in love relationships, but the same effects are created by other relationships of less intensity. A long-term relationship with someone at work, the ongoing camaraderie or rivalry with a brother or a sister, a relationship between you and your parents—changes in any of these or similar relationships have the potential to create strong emotions and significant side effects in your life.

We have learned that changes in relationships can be dealt with more effectively if the individuals involved are clearly aware that old programs and strong emotions often do everything they can to take over.

The key to overcoming this problem for yourself is to begin by taking a closer look at your own response to relationship changes in your past, and to start to see how you might improve those responses in the future. The answer lies in your choice to get better at doing it—and in beginning to *practice* every chance you get.

■

■   **PERSONAL EXERCISES**   ■

1. Rate yourself (1 through 10) on the level that you are able to successfully manage your emotions during an important change in any of the following personal relationships. (A 1 is little or no self-control; a 10 is high self-management.)
   a. With husband/wife _____
   b. With a parent _____
   c. With a son or daughter _____
   d. With a close friend _____
   e. With someone at work _____
   f. With a romantic partner _____

2. Who (or what) do you feel is actually in control of most of the changes that take place in your relationships?

_____

3. What other important issues do you deal with when you are experiencing a change in your relationship? (Examples: change in life-style, dealing with opinions of others, how you feel about yourself.)
   a. _____
   b. _____
   c. _____
   d. _____
   e. _____

4. In dealing with a change in a relationship, what personal styles or actions do you adopt that work against you?
   a. _____
   b. _____
   c. _____

5. *In dealing with a change in a relationship, what personal styles or actions do you adopt that work for you?*

a. _____

b. _____

c. _____

6. *As we have seen, most changes in relationships are more difficult to deal with because of the emotions involved. In order to take a step back from your emotions and allow your logical mind to help you deal with the change more effectively, use the following exercise the next time you are facing a change in an important relationship:*

Ask someone you trust—a close friend or your spouse or mate (someone in a neutral position)—to sit down with you and set aside a minimum of thirty minutes to talk. Then regarding the relationship change you are dealing with, have your friend ask you the question:

a. *"In dealing with this relationship, what result do you most want to create?"*

Start your answer by saying, "In dealing with this relationship, the result I most want to create is . . ." and then finish the sentence and go on from there. Say everything you have to say that you can think of about the result that you really want to create. After you're through talking, your friend is to ask you the same question again:

b. *"In dealing with this relationship, what result do you most want to create?"*

Answer the question again. This time, your answer may be a little different. It will probably be a little more focused. Begin the answer by saying, "In dealing with this relationship, the result that I most want to create is . . ." and then talk. When you are through, and when you have said everything you have to say, your friend is to ask you the same question a third time:

c. *"In dealing with this relationship, what result do you most want to create?"*

Once again, begin your answer by saying, "In dealing with this relationship, the result that I most want to create is . . ." and then continue talking.

The first time or two that you answer the question, you may be dealing with the outer layers of what you want, but it is usually only after you have answered the question as completely as possible several times in a row that you finally begin to strip away the outer layers and get down to who you really are and what you really want.

Try the same technique with any of the other questions that are asked in Chapter 13. The more you know about yourself and what you really stand to gain from this change, the more you will give yourself the opportunity to excel because of it.

10

A Change in Your Personal Direction

A *change in direction* is one of the most important changes you or I could ever face. And yet, it is a change that most of us will go through at least once and sometimes several times in our lives.

A change in direction means a change in goals. It is when we move from one focus to another. A change in direction can be anything from a change in careers to a change in interests to a change in life-style to a change in how we think about things. A change in direction can be as small as a change in how we spend our time, or as grand a change as the finding of a new meaning in life.

Some changes in direction happen almost automatically; they are the result of growing up and making our way through the predetermined changes that we must go through from youth to adulthood to family, career, and beyond.

Of all of the Major Changes it is the change called *direction* that can be—and should be—one of the most rewarding changes we will encounter. This is one of the changes that should always work *for* us instead of *against* us. But like the other Major Changes we have discussed, this change, too, is one that should be recognized and dealt with, with the utmost of care.

Changes in direction mean changes in purpose, in attitudes, and in actions. It is when we set new sights and change our path, when we make sweeping changes in what we think about and what we do. Of all the changes that we have mentioned here, it is this one change—the change of personal direction—that holds within it the potential for the most widespread changes in the rest of our lives.

Another reason that a change in direction is set apart from the other changes we make is that it is one change that we usually must decide to make for ourselves. A true change in direction almost never comes from the outside, to be forced upon us. People and events outside of us can influence our decision to make a change in direction, but finally the decision to do so gets down to what *we* want or agree to.

In some cases, a change in direction is brought about by some event that we had not planned for; in other cases, the change in direction that falls upon us comes almost entirely by our own previous path—the steps we have taken in the past. Sometimes when a change of direction comes, it seems to be an accident of life, and we are convinced to change what we are doing or how we spend our time.

Let's imagine what it might look like if we could actually see the coming of change in the form of a messenger of change—and in so doing learn to see the messenger for what it really represents.

I'll illustrate this point with a story about a man named Kenneth, who is about to face one of the Seven Major Changes. And in this story, we will, along with Ken, be able to recognize the messenger of change when it arrives. This is just one example out of dozens that we might see taking place in our own lives or in the lives of people we know. One day, something just like this could apply to any of us.

■ *The Story of Kenneth*

Kenneth locked the front door, closed the screen door behind him, and stepped out onto the front steps and into the cool night air. He had agreed to attend a retirement party at his friend Alvin's house a few blocks away. Ken's wife had gone on ahead to help get ready for the party, and Kenneth had decided to walk to Alvin's home.

During the past few years Kenneth had made a point of keeping himself in shape. "Age isn't everything," he had often told himself, and Kenneth believed it. He still thought like someone twenty years younger than he was. He felt good about his health, and he liked the fact that he could look in the mirror at himself in the morning and still see someone who had not let himself go. Besides, Kenneth had to keep in shape. His wife Evie was eight years younger than he was, and she, too, was still going strong. Evie worked as a receptionist in the front office of the power company's executive offices, where she had been almost as long as Kenneth had been superintendent.

As he walked along the tree-lined street where he and Evie lived, Kenneth felt pretty good. The party he was attending was a surprise party for his old friend Rudy, who was retiring the next week at the end of fifteen years of service at the same plant where Kenneth worked.

Kenneth had started at the plant earlier than Rudy, and had risen higher, but he didn't give a lot of thought to his own pending retirement. "When the time comes, the time will come," he told himself whenever he did think about it. "I've got too much to do today to worry about that kind of thing."

Kenneth was walking at his usual brisk pace along the street toward the house where the party was being held, when someone stepped out from under the street light and joined in step with him. Kenneth was surprised at first, and then, as he saw who it was, he was delighted.

The young man who had joined him was his youngest son, Todd, who was twenty-eight and one of his best friends. "I knew you were going to Rudy's retirement party, and I thought I'd walk along with you. I think we need to talk," Todd said.

"What is it you'd like to talk about?" Ken asked. He really liked talking with Todd, but he did have a party to attend, and he had to be there by eight o'clock sharp, when they would be bringing the cake out for Rudy and everyone would join in singing "For He's a Jolly Good Fellow." Kenneth didn't want to miss that.

"Dad, you're about to go through an important change in your life, and because I care a lot about you, I want you to be ready," his son said.

When he heard that, Kenneth really didn't want to listen, but he did. In fact, nothing could have torn him away from what his son was beginning to say. "For most of your life you have followed one direction, and now that direction has to change." Kenneth hoped Todd wasn't talking to him about the word "retirement," but he sensed that he was—and Todd's next words confirmed it.

"You've worked hard your whole life so that someday you could retire," Todd continued. "I've heard you talk about it a lot, and I know you've looked forward to it for a long time—but I couldn't help noticing that anytime the conversation got too specific about just *when* you would retire, the subject somehow got changed. I know it's difficult to think about all the changes in your life that retirement means—and I've seen you try not to think about it. But Dad, I'm afraid you may not have prepared yourself for it as well as you might have."

For the next ten or fifteen minutes, as they walked along together, Todd and Kenneth talked about the days ahead when Ken would have to leave his job at the plant and make a new life for himself and create a new and different relationship with everything in his life, even with Evie.

"Very little will be the same," Todd said, "and most of how you think it's going to be won't be that way at all. That's because you haven't practiced living without your work. You have only gotten away from it now and then, but you couldn't wait to get back to it. But now you'll have to find something to keep you going, a way of living that helps you live and keeps you from dying."

These were somber words for Kenneth to hear. The more he listened to his son talk, and the more he thought about the celebration he was about to attend that evening, the more he realized that he didn't envy his friend Rudy at all. As they walked and as they talked, the picture in Ken's mind of what he would one day have to face for himself was starting to become clear for the first time in his life.

He saw himself sitting home alone in the big old empty house with Evie still getting up and singing her cheerful morning songs each morning, and then watching her get in the car and drive off to her job at the same plant where Kenneth would no longer be welcome in the same way himself. Kenneth saw himself still seeing his friends from work, and getting together with them down at Sir Winston's now and then for some darts and a beer, but he knew that they wouldn't treat him quite the same. After all, he wouldn't be the same, would he? He would be different. He wouldn't be a part of the team. Kenneth would be on the outside looking in. He would be *retired*.

Kenneth and his son now stood at the door of his friend's home, where the retirement party was about to begin. Kenneth was on time by just a minute or two, and as he rang the bell, Todd stood beside him.

Ken was just beginning to wonder whether anyone was going to answer the bell, when the doors were flung open wide—and there, gathered together in the front room of his friend's home was what looked like everyone Kenneth could remember ever having met from work; there were even friends from his bowling team and members of Kenneth's congregation at church.

And then the song burst forth and the multitude of friends in front of him, their faces glowing with happy excitement, in close unison began to sing the words of the song, "For He's a Jolly Good Fellow." And there, right in front, stood Evie. Her cheeks were flushed with excitement and happiness for the moment. She looked for all the world exactly like she did when she was seventeen years old, when she had surprised him with a birthday party. And when he looked into those wonderful sparkling eyes, he thought he saw something that looked like tears.

As the gathered crowd parted and the giant cake was wheeled toward Kenneth, he turned and smiled, and then nodded his head in understanding toward his son, Todd, who had been so caring in his delivery of the difficult message of change he had been responsible for giving to his father.

Ken now understood; it was his own retirement party, not Rudy's. It marked the end of Ken's long career; for Kenneth, the change called *direction* had arrived.

■ *The Change That Offers So Much Good*

A change in direction is almost always at the same time a challenge and an opportunity. But the overriding strength of this one major change is that the gain almost always exceeds the challenge.

Of all the Major Changes, it is a change in personal direction that captures our entire attention. A change in direction is like a very personal and fundamental change within us. It isn't just a part of us that changes direction. A change in direction represents a change in our *lives*. And a change in our lives usually gets our full attention.

Here are some other changes in direction. On the following list, you will probably find changes in direction that either you or someone you know has gone through.

- Graduation from school or college
- A new job
- A new career path
- Getting married
- Religious conversion
- Undergoing open-heart surgery
- Undergoing a major emotional or spiritual crisis or awakening
- Having children
- Getting divorced
- Retirement
- Going back to school
- Reaching a major goal
- An unexpected change in your personal or family finances
- Associating with a new friend or a new group of friends
- Achieving a major accomplishment
- Reaching a point of dissatisfaction with your life
- Setting major *new* goals

There are clearly a lot of situations that can lead to new directions. What is more important to recognize, however, is that those same situations can create either positive new directions or downturns for your future, depending on how you deal with the change itself, and how solid your goals are.

■ *Your Direction is Ultimately up to You*

Whatever event brings the Major Change of *direction*, determining your direction should never be left in the hands of someone else. What you do with the rest of your life—wherever you are at now—should always be up to you. After all, you're the one responsible for living your life, and no one else can ever live your life for you. That's the basis of taking personal responsibility for yourself; you cannot excel if you are trying to live your life based on someone else's script. And that includes trying to live up to or down to someone else's expectations or demands. It is what you expect of yourself that counts the most. It is what *you* demand of *you* that should determine the direction that you choose to follow.

When the change called *direction* pays you a visit, it may surprise you or you may have been expecting the change for a long time. In either case, what happens *next*—the direction you follow—should be a direction of your own making, instead of one that does nothing more than react to an outside influence as though you were powerless to do anything about it.

■ *The Two Kinds of Change in Your Personal Direction*

The first kind of change in direction is one you predetermine for yourself; you set up the change in advance, so you know what you are doing. You are planning the change yourself, and you are anticipating the results.

With this type of change in direction, you keep yourself in control of what is happening to you. Even if everything doesn't go exactly according to your plan, at least you *have* a plan, and you have something by which to monitor your progress. Unlike Kenneth, who may have wanted to put off dealing with his retirement, when dealing with a change in personal direction it is a much safer bet to set detailed goals, outline a specific plan of action, learn everything you can about the change and its consequences—and even get some practice feeling what the new direction will be like once it has arrived.

The second type of change is the unexpected kind. A major heart attack or critical surgery can herald a change that no one really expects or believes is going to happen until it does. That is a change in direction that is unexpected, and difficult or impossible to plan for.

Another example of an unexpected change in direction might be when for some reason your job suddenly disappears; you are happily engaged in your work one day and out of a job the next. And there are many people who have said that the day their husband or wife walked out on them, they had no idea that it was about to happen to them.

Those kinds of surprise circumstances do have the power to suddenly change our individual direction in life. But in many cases, the change is unexpected more because the individual unconsciously *denied* its possibility than because the change was truly a surprise that could not have been predicted.

It is easy for us to become so preoccupied with the daily business of living that we fail to keep in close touch with an important part of our inner selves. And so we don't listen. We are not vigilant, and we blind ourselves to the signs that tell us something big is coming—and that *something* is going to change the rest of our life.

It is usually after we are thrown off our feet that we are most apt to say that we should have seen it coming. The aware person learns to see it coming before it arrives. He learns that survival means more than making ends meet or keeping up with the Joneses. He becomes aware of a higher calling, a recognition of his own potential, and the responsibility to live up to the highest level of his true inner nature. So he listens to his inner mind. He consciously practices keeping in touch with who he really is and with the truth of what is really happening around him.

That is the person who is seldom caught off guard. That is the person who is the most likely to set the goals, work at them, and change his direction by personal design.

▪

▪ **PERSONAL EXERCISES** ▪

1. After discussing this exercise with your closest friend or clearly thinking it through on your own, in just one sentence each, write a statement defining the three most important directions in your life right now:

(1) _____

(2) _____

(3) _____

2. Next, write out who or what is most in control of maintaining or changing each of these three directions:

(1) _____

(2) _____

(3) _____

3. Name the one most important change in direction in your life that you would like to work on now.

_____

4. What other changes will you initiate or create by this change in direction?

a. _____

b. _____

c. _____

_____

11

A Change in
Your Health

If the next Major Change—
a *change in health*—were to pay a visit, it would
bring one of two kinds of change in someone's health:
either the change brought on by illness or a *problem*
with health, or a change toward *good* health—getting
healthier!

Both of these changes in health can create paramount changes in attitude, energy, and mobility. To see
the results of this kind of change, all you have to do is
spend time with someone who has recently become ill
or someone who has just spent three months in a total
fitness program. In both cases, the change in the status
of their health creates noticeable and sometimes far-
reaching changes in many other areas of their lives.

Most of us have known someone who went
through a long-term illness or faced some other physical trauma. When we see that happen, the other

changes that the physical problem creates are obvious. Just as there is nothing like starting a new day off feeling good, it is also true that there is nothing quite like starting each day having to cope with illness or a downturn in physical health. It affects our entire outlook.

It is in the area of health and wellness that we can be especially thankful for rapid technological and scientific advances. Our fast-changing world has created fast-changing developments in the field of medicine and health. We have come a long way in a very short period of time. There are still people living today who remember when there was little more than aspirin and tonic to treat an illness—no matter what was wrong with them.

Those same people must be astonished now when they think about CAT scans and PET scans that let doctors look inside the brain without even touching it, or when they consider the pharmacological magic that has given us an armory of drugs that treat everything from life-shortening high blood pressure to advanced cases of schizophrenia, or when they hear of interartery laser surgery techniques that give new life to people who would have otherwise had shorter lives because of a malfunctioning heart.

The same individuals who saw firsthand the crippling and deadly effects of polio, as an example, now have access to modern medical miracles that allow them to receive new hearts and lungs and kidneys. They have learned of neurological techniques that save countless lives because doctors can now understand the intricate neuroanatomy of the human brain. They have seen wonderful developments in the field of neuromuscular treatment that allow the lame to walk and gives life back to limbs that once would have been useless. And all of these advances in medicine are the result of our fast-changing world.

However, the same technology that is giving us more answers and more actual day-to-day solutions that help us enhance the quality of our lives also seems to create many of the difficulties that we now have to live with. Even though technology makes many miracles possible, it has also brought more complications and problems. We are faced with moral dilemmas, emotional hardships, and choices we have never had before. The fast-changing advances in medicine affect more than our physical well-being.

At the same time we have rediscovered the notion of *fitness*. It is becoming popular to make good health and physical fitness a way of life. We are learning to see exercise as a positive tool to help us feel better and live longer. We are changing the way we view food and what we eat. No longer is it okay or popular to think of a diet of meat and potatoes (and the high levels of fat and cholesterol and sodium that go along with it) as a standard diet to be fed to hardworking parents and active kids.

While a growing number of available cable channels on the television set tries to seduce us into spending more and more leisure time hours watching programs on TV, we have also discovered the value of using leisure time for positive physical sports and recreation. We are learning to participate in sports instead of just watching them on the screen. Fitness centers, tennis courts, bicycle paths, and running trails have become increasingly popular due to our growing attempts to create a healthier life-style.

■ How Do You Deal with a Downturn in Health?

Yet in spite of the wonderful medical advances of the 20th century, a breakdown in physical health of any kind and for whatever reason can still cause calamity in our lives. We're getting better at fixing the problems, but for now there are many personal health problems that still remain with us.

If sickness, poor health, or some physical calamity comes your way, it will still be in *how you deal with it* that will, at least in part, determine the result it will create for you in the other areas of your life. Your medical doctor will probably tell you that your own attitude can play a vital role in your success in dealing with a problem of personal health.

There is a great deal to be encouraged about; a lot of good things are happening. But you will still have to decide for yourself whether you are going to let a health problem get you down or defeat you—or if you are going to rise above it.

■ Controlling the Related Changes

We are not at the point yet where we can turn every physical setback into a medical triumph. But we are getting better at turning the problems of health from major defeats into personal victories. It would be insensitive for me to suggest that the final solution to any ongoing problem with your own personal health could be resolved or even significantly lessened merely by telling yourself that you are going to make the best of it. And yet, there are so many stories of lives that have been filled with the achievement of overcoming potential physical problems or defeats—of people who rose above the difficulties by the simple fact that they *chose* to do so.

Dealing with our own health, or the lack of it, can represent a real challenge to any of us. But it is those who choose to move forward, and excel in their lives in spite of the changes in their health, that have the best chance of living with the problem successfully or defeating it entirely.

Some people, when they become ill or physically disabled, spend most of their time complaining about the problem and commiserating with others. Yet there are people who deal with the *same* situation by finding a more positive approach to the problem. Instead of dwelling on the misfortune of the problem itself, they focus on other people who have not only gotten through it but have gained something because of it.

There is a healthy tone to that approach. When a problem occurs that affects our health or affects us physically in any way, the truth is this: We can either do something about it or we can't. If we *can* do something about the problem, we should exercise every resource that is available to us.

If the problem with our health is such that we have done everything we can and there is nothing else we can do, then it gets down to a matter of our own perspective and attitude. It is almost always those who choose to do the best they possibly can in spite of it who end up doing the best. It is a matter of choice, and it is a matter of resolve. When the sixth messenger of change called *health* arrives, and the news he brings is not the best, then overcoming it will be up to you and what you choose to do next.

■ *The Other Kind of Change in Health*

There is the other side of dealing with health in a positive way that we are learning not to ignore—in fact, we are learning to take advantage of it. That is the choice to create more health and more wellness for yourself. This has to do with diet and exercise and lifestyle—and above all, it has to do with making the personal *decision* to be healthy. Getting healthy, feeling fit, and feeling in control of yourself and your habits can create some exceptionally positive changes in your life. They are the kinds of changes that we should all look forward to having to deal with.

If this major change were to visit you, I suspect that you would choose to have the change caused by your personal decision to get wonderfully and positively healthy in every way. The changes that decision could make are *always* easier to deal with. Choosing to live at your best—mentally, spiritually, personally, and physically—is a goal that no sensible person would ever want to question.

■

■ PERSONAL EXERCISES ■

1. What one word best describes your most typical attitude about a problem with your health? _____

2. Rate (1 to 10) how well you feel you deal with a negative change in your health (a 1 is very poorly; a 10 is very well). _____

3. Write out three realistic personal goals about your health. After each goal, write two things that you can do to achieve that goal.

(1) My first goal about my health is:
_____
_____

My action steps are:
(a) _____
(b) _____
(c) _____

(2) My second goal about my health is:
_____
_____

My action steps are:
(a) _____
(b) _____
(c) _____

(3) My third goal about my health is:
_____
_____

My action steps are:
(a) _____
(b) _____
(c) _____

12

Personal Growth— A Change in *You*

Let's look at another example of someone who meets a messenger of change. In this story, too, we will be able to see the messenger of change arrive, as though it were a person that we could actually talk to, and learn from. We might not have experienced some of the troubles that Alex went through, but if you look deep, there is sometimes a shadow of Alexander in each of us.

▪ *The Story of Alexander*

For Alexander, who stood staring down into the deep, rushing waters beneath the bridge, the sky could not have been darker or the day more forlorn. Alexander no longer even thought about trying to make himself feel better. He had lost so much that he had started to believe that it was other people who got to have lives that worked, but not him.

Just a year and a half ago Alexander had gotten married for the third time—and this time the marriage had worked. He could not have found a more loving and caring companion and wife than Christine. After he and Christine were married, Alex lived some of the happiest days he had ever known.

Alexander had found the happiness he was looking for, and a relationship that worked. And so he nurtured the relationship and worked to help it grow, and he knew that the happiness he had finally found would last.

Then one night Christine didn't come home from work. It was just a week and a half before Christmas. Alexander was away from home, working on a construction project and staying overnight at a small motel, when he called home and there was no one there to answer the phone. After three more calls, the worry he felt had turned to fear. To try to calm himself, Alex told himself that Christine must have gone Christmas shopping and stayed out longer than she had expected.

By eight-thirty Alexander couldn't bear the worry and the strain any longer, and he checked out of the motel, and headed for home. He would never forget that drive home. It was filled with hope and prayer and an endless stream of pictures of his wonderful, precious Christine that ran through his mind.

Alexander arrived at his house at 10:35 p.m. As he ran up the steps to the side door that led into the kitchen, he could hear the telephone ringing inside, and without the porch light, he fumbled at the keyhole in the doorknob. Finally it turned, and he was inside, gasping for breath and saying "Hello—Christine?" into the telephone. But instead of Christine's voice on the phone, it was Christine's mother, and she was crying. There had been a car accident and Christine had been killed.

Whatever Alexander had thought about life's meaning before that day, now it began to change forever.

He began to wall himself off from everyone and everything. Two days after Christine's funeral Alexander went back to work, but he would talk to almost no one. Then there were times when he wouldn't show up for work at all. Many of the people where he worked were his friends, and they did what they could to help, but there was little they could do. Anything they said to Alex was met with an empty, lifeless stare. It was as though Alex had gone somewhere else and left only the shell of his body and mind behind.

Even before he finally lost his job, Alex had started to take long, aimless walks by himself. He didn't seem to have any particular direction in mind, or plan for where he was going, but he usually ended up standing on the bridge and looking down into the water below.

"I should never have been born," Alex thought, and even as he thought it, in a far-distant recess of his mind he could hear his own father saying those same words to him when he could not have been more than two or three years old. "Sometimes I wish you had never been born!" his father would yell at him. "You were never supposed to be here in the first place!"

Somehow the words had stuck, and somehow they had come true. Over the years, Alex had worked very hard to doubt those words and to fight them. He had been determined to prove that he was better than that, and that he did have value, and that he was worthwhile, and above all, that there was reason and purpose in his life and that he *did* have a reason for being here.

But with enough failure and enough disappointment and even broken dreams—and then the blow of losing Christine, Alexander had finally fallen slowly to his knees, prepared to give up the fight for good.

It was then, as Alexander stood alone on the bridge and decided that he could not go on, that a messenger of change in the form of an old fisherman introduced Alexander to the change called *personal growth*.

Alex was standing there at the railing, thinking of his defeat, when he felt a hand on his shoulder, and he turned. There, standing beside him, was the white-haired old fisherman he had often seen fishing from the bridge. "I don't want to talk," Alexander said. "That is true," the old man answered him, "but I think it's time. It's none of my business, but I've seen you here a lot lately, and it's starting to look like you might think it's the end of the world."

It may be that the only reason Alexander listened to the old man was because it didn't seem to matter *what* happened to him next. He no longer wanted to live, and he was no longer afraid of dying—so as he saw it, there wasn't much that could happen to him that could possibly make any difference to him at all. So when this messenger of change began to speak, Alexander listened almost indifferently, not knowing and not really caring what would come next.

"It looks like you are about to go through a great change in your life," the old man began. "What you have thought to be the end of your life will soon become its beginning." Alex looked at the stranger curiously, with some skepticism in his eyes, and perhaps some curiosity. "I don't think I know what you're talking about," he said.

"What you thought was meaningless before will

have more meaning now than you have ever known," the old man said. "In what you thought was worthless, you will find great value. What you believed had no reason will now have purpose. What you knew as failure and defeat you will now know as success and victory."

"What are you talking about?" Alexander asked. "What meaning? What value? What purpose? What success, what victory? What are you talking about?" And then the messenger of change looked straight into Alexander's eyes and spoke very clearly. "I am talking about *you*," he said.

"When you were young," the messenger continued, "you were told many things about yourself. You were told that you would fail, and that you had no reason to exist. You were told that you had no value or worth, and that your life had no purpose. You were told many things about yourself and you believed them to be true. You are now going to learn that none of them were. For all this time you have listened to the voice that told you what you *could not do* and what you *could not become* in your life, and for all this time you have been listening to the wrong voice. *None of what you were told is true.*"

"But it *was* true, every word of it!" Alexander interrupted. "I *have* failed. Nothing that I ever did that was worth anything lasted," he said. "And look at me now—I have nothing! I have nothing to show for anything good that I have ever done. My whole life has been wasted trying to win and never really winning anything."

"I suppose that would be true," the messenger said, "if at this moment you climbed over this railing and let yourself drop into the water. Then we would never hear from you again, and your belief in your own failure would have been true. That would be the only loss. That would be a life without purpose. But my reason for talking to you now is not to show you what you have lost; it is to show you what you have gained."

For more than an hour the old man talked—and Alexander listened. And in that time, as the messenger of change spoke to him, Alexander began to see a new picture of himself being formed in his mind. "You are only and always everything that you believe yourself to be," the messenger said. "It is not what you would like to be that matters most. *It is what you choose to believe as truth about yourself that forms and shapes the person you will become.* All this time you have wanted to believe in something better for yourself, but instead of believing in yourself you chose to pattern your life after the misbeliefs of someone else—and *you made them come true.*

"The truth is," the old man said, "that the trials you have faced in finding yourself were not defeats at all. Each one of them, if you now choose to accept it, has taught you many things. They were more than lessons about life, those you could learn from a book. They were lessons about *you*, and those are the lessons that you cannot learn by reading or listening to others. Let me show you now what you have learned."

As the messenger of change talked on, word by word and thought by thought, Alexander began to see a different picture of himself. Everything in his past that had seemed to work so hard to conspire against him began to take on a new and different meaning as the old man talked. What Alexander had believed for years to be nothing but pitfalls and problems and proof of his failings, the old man began to show as the awakening of new potentials.

As the beginning of Alexander's new awareness

started to sink in and take hold, the messenger of change continued. "If you want to find your potential, and if you choose to excel in your life, *never again listen to the words from your past that told you what you could not be.* From this day onward, listen only to those words from yourself that give you the future and the promise that you are destined to achieve. I cannot begin to tell you the many wonderful things that are about to happen in your life now.

"When you reawaken and begin to come back to life, everything you see and everything you hear, and even what you think, will have a new sense of life to it. When you begin to believe in yourself, you begin to see almost everything differently, and nothing will be quite the same anymore. The awakening you are about to experience can happen to anyone—and it can happen to you."

And then, once again, the old man turned to Alexander and looked into his eyes. In a voice of wisdom and knowing, he said the final words of his message. "Young man, you are not a person without purpose or reason. You are not created to fail, and you never were. You were given from birth the crown of success and the scepter of greatness. You are a person of quality and value and goodness and worth. Live well, my friend; your life awaits you."

■ There Is No Reason That We Cannot Grow

There is no telling what you can bring to life in your own future when you recognize that the messenger of change, of *personal growth*, calls on you. No matter what has gone on in the past in your own life, there is so much to gain, so much progress to make!

There have been books upon books written on the subject of personal growth. They talk to us about *enlightenment* of one kind or another, and they tell us, much as the messenger of change told Alexander, that it is the simple step of becoming *aware* that, when given the chance, opens the door for us to our own futures. Many of those books have helped a lot of their readers get the point and recognize how often they stand at the crossroads of their lives.

When people hear that message, some of them—a few of them—seize the moment and make the choice. They make the decision to see their past as positive experiences, put the difficulties and the traumas behind them, and get on with their lives. That is the response that the recognition of personal growth is intended to create.

Yet, there are many other people who, even when they learn the truth about personal growth, will do nothing at all about it. Over the years I have been asked many times why some people find themselves and strive to reach their potential while most others let it slide and put it off for another day or another time in their lives—or do nothing about it at all.

My answer has been this: It is because the programming we received in our past holds such strong control in our lives now that we are unable to get past it. The result is that the control of our own futures is often out of our hands. There are ways to change the old programs, but even knowing that, most people will do nothing about it. It is as though those who don't, because of their old and untrue past programming, do not have the will to take control and actually *practice* changing their lives for the better. Perhaps the Major

Change called *personal growth* has come calling—but they are not yet listening.

■ *We Don't Have to Wait for the Messenger of Change*

Although some of what Alexander had to deal with in his life is not unlike what many of us experience ourselves, it does not have to take a roller-coaster ride of challenges and defeats to get us to the point that we are ready to finally make a breakthrough. It does seem, however, that it sometimes takes trauma or defeat to get us to the point that we are shaken out of our complacency.

The most important message that the messenger of change that brings personal growth can give us is this: When it comes to making the choice to make personal growth a part of our lives, we would do better if we did not wait for the messenger to come calling. We are intelligent enough that we should not have to live a life in which personal growth or what is called "self-discovery" is forced upon us. We are smart enough to recognize its value for ourselves.

As we will learn, much of what we call personal growth is in fact the result of having faced changes directly, and dealt with them successfully. In the following chapters we will be discussing specific steps that will help you recognize the opportunity of personal growth *before* it upsets your life or causes problems by its arrival.

∎ Take Control of Your Own Personal Growth

In many ways, the story of Alexander is a true story that happens in different ways in the lives of all of us. We may not have to suffer a series of difficulties or defeats to arrive at that point, and all of us may not have received the terribly poor programming that Alexander received as a child. But in one way or another, the opportunity for personal growth arrives, and the choice to grow or not grow is left up to each of us.

In a way, however, we can almost wish that the same messenger of change who called on Alexander would knock on our door and show us our own more positive futures. But then, if we listen carefully, I suspect that the messenger is at the door and waiting to talk to us more often than we know.

Watching the change of personal growth, and feeling it wake us up and bring us to life, should not have to be something that happens only now and then. It should happen to us every day that we choose to chase the darker clouds away and see the beauty and brightness of the life that is in front of us. The old man is right. It can happen to anyone, and it can happen to you.

■

■ PERSONAL EXERCISES ■

1. *Rate (1 to 10) the actual importance to you of creating recognizable personal growth in your own life (a 1 is least important; a 10 is most important):* _____

2. *List three important things that you would like to do that would bring the change of personal growth to your life now or in the future:*

a. _____

b. _____

c. _____

3. *Who or what do you believe is in control of your personal growth?* _____

4. *Do you believe that personal growth is:*

a. *The result of circumstances* _____

b. *The objective of a predetermined goal* _____

c. *Other* _____

5. *Take some time to think about this question. What you really believe about your own meaning and potential in life will ultimately and always determine your level of success or failure. This next self-statement will help you evaluate and determine your deepest personal feelings about your right to achieve a high level of personal growth in your life. Complete the statement:*

"I honestly believe that among people who deserve to achieve their greatest personal potential, I would rate myself as being:

a. *Not destined to achieve."* _____

b. *Average."* _____

c. *Above average."* _____

d. *Destined to achieve exceptional potential in my life."* _____

If you answered a, b, or c to this question, it may be helpful for you to pay special attention to Chapter 23, "Metamorphosis—Getting Ready to Make It Work," and the section entitled "Living Through Change with Incredible You" in particular.

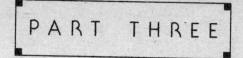

PART THREE

Developing a Strategy

13

The Questions
of Change

The questions in this chapter can apply to any important change you are dealing with. A summary of these questions, with spaces for you to fill in your own answers, appears in Chapter 26, "Your Personal Book of Changes."

As you read the questions that follow, identify the *specific change* that you want to give attention to, and apply each of the questions to that area of change in your life:

1. Is the change something that happened in the past, or is it happening now, in the present?

Anytime you are working at dealing with any important change, ask yourself this question: Is this a problem that has *already* happened, or is it happening to you *now*? Is it current, or at least recent? There may be a message in the answer you give yourself. Some changes create such a severe shock that some people can't let go of them. Other changes become so paramount in the person's life that even in time, the person is *unwilling* to let go of them.

A man I know, whom I will call Edward, suffered the loss of his daughter, Jennifer, when she was in her early twenties. The loss tore Edward and his family apart. The unreasonableness of Jennifer's death was too much for Edward to understand, too much for him to take. Not only was the entire future, the whole world, of his young daughter lost, but so was Edward's faith in nearly everything he had ever believed in. The unfairness of it all made no sense, and trying to work through his anguish, he soon began to commit every moment of days and then weeks and then months and eventually years, to a personal quest to find meaning and value and purpose in that loss.

The loss of his daughter became the singular motivating force in Edward's life. It was as though the sacrifice of his own self could somehow bring back the life that Jennifer had lost. The loss and everything that loss meant became the central theme of Edward's existence.

I would not suggest how this man should live his own life—not a moment of it. He chose to do with his time what he believed to be right for himself. But many people do the same, and then much later something happens—and they wake up one day and have themselves back again. What is important about this is not what those people say while they are hanging on to the loss. It is what they say when they finally come back to life. They often say, "Why did I take so long to get through it? I hung on too long; I stopped living myself!"

The same thing can be said for careers that were

lost, marriages that ended in divorce, homes that were left behind, and even dreams that were lost—but were never forgotten.

2. Is the change *certain* to happen, is it only *"possible,"* or could it just be *imagined*?

Ask yourself this question when you are looking at any important change in your life *that has not yet happened*. If the change is *certain* to happen—if there is no avoiding it—you usually know. If you are realistic, you know if the coming change is absolutely *real*—or if it isn't.

Yet many of us have a built-in "doubter's program" that causes us to fear the worst—when there may be no real likelihood of the worst actually happening. We know that we shouldn't hide our heads and ignore something that we ought to be prepared for, but the problem is that we can spend more time worrying about an event *that will never happen*—than we would actually spend dealing with the event if it *did* happen.

We have all heard the adages about unnecessary time wasted on worry; most of the worry never comes true. But when you're learning to deal with change effectively, the subject of unnecessary worry becomes even more important. The reason for this is that when you are worrying about something that has not happened—and very possibly will not happen—you are spending some of your most valuable time and mental energy fighting the wrong battle! That would be like the knights of old defending the *empty* castle, and leaving the *other* castle—the one with the king and the queen and the beautiful princess inside—undefended.

Each of us has only so much time and so much mental and emotional energy. If you use yours up slaying invisible dragons, you may have nothing left to fight with when the real dragon comes along. Building your energy, keeping yourself sharp, alert, positive and healthy, and full of spiritual vitality, is a good strategy. Defeating yourself by fighting worries in the dark is not.

3. Is this change temporary, or is it permanent?

Is this change something that is going to last forever, or is it short-term?

One of the guidelines that determines how well we can deal with a change is how long we think it will *last*. If the change that is taking place is not going to last beyond your endurance or patience, you probably find it easier to say, "This is okay. This too shall pass."

If the change is *not* going to pass, then it is important to recognize that and *plan* for it. Learning to excel in a time of change is not built on hopes and wishes. It is built on a knowledge of what is going on and what is really happening, and having a solid workable plan to deal with it.

4. Who or what is in control of the *effects* of this change now?

Notice that the question is not "Who or what is in control of the *change itself*?" but rather, "What is controlling the underlying *results*—the outcome of the change?" What is responsible for whether this change is creating a *positive* result in your life or a *negative* result?

The objective is to put *yourself* in charge of the effects that this change is having on you. You may not be responsible for the change taking place, but it is always up to you to take (or not take) responsibility for how any change ends up affecting you.

In the earlier story of Katherine (the change of separation), it was clear that she had successfully gotten through the changes caused by the loss of her husband. It also looked like there was a very good chance that Katherine would deal equally well with the newer change of separation from her working lifestyle.

We didn't know precisely what she was going to do next, but we could be quite certain that the next step she took would be a positive move, even if it was to request a change in her job status or some other alternative plan. We had the feeling that Katherine was about to put herself in control of the effects of the change instead of letting the change itself control the rest of her life for her.

People who practice taking responsibility for themselves are the most successful at dealing with change. They should be; they've learned to deal with life in a personally mature and responsible way.

People who do *not* practice taking responsibility for themselves deal with change less successfully. For them, there is always a blame to lay on someone else's shoulders. To them, life is often unfair and unjust. So they see themselves as being singled out, placed on the list of those destined to have troublesome lives, and they spend their time and their energies living in a zone of negativity, fighting change with complaint instead of finding its advantages.

Who or what is in control of the effects of any important change in your life now? The one who is firmly in control of the effects that this change is having on you should be *you* and no one else.

5. Is there a way to minimize any negative effects of the change?

A good first answer to this question is *yes!*

If you and I were to sit down and talk about a specific change that is happening in your life right now, this is one of the questions we would discuss. I suspect that together we would come up with quite a list of things that you could do to turn the potentially negative effects of this change into some very practical positives.

Write down nine or ten ideas in answer to that question and watch what that one activity can do to your sense of well-being when you're trying to make the best of dealing with a change.

In several of the following chapters we will be discussing specific steps that you can take to minimize any negative effects that could come from a change you're dealing with.

6. What do you stand to lose because of this change?

What do you stand to lose—*really*? Sort through your thoughts on this, and separate the list of things you actually stand to *lose* because of the change from the list of things that you just don't *like* about it.

By doing this, you may learn that you will not necessarily lose anything of real value to you because of the change. Much of our reaction to change is based on insecurity or fear of the unknown. It is often easier for us not to change. So it can *feel* like the change is taking something away from us, when what it is really taking away is our sense of security.

When nothing is changing we may have the feeling that we are safe and we are losing nothing. But it is when nothing is changing that we may be going nowhere. The greatest losses do not come from change; the greatest losses come from not moving forward.

7. What do you stand to gain from this change?

In a later chapter about creating the right internal

attitudes to deal with change, we will discuss how much of your attitude is actually your choice. I know people who are conditioned to automatically look at any change that they did not want to have happen as being all negative. Their first—and sometimes only—reaction to the change is that it is bad, and that they have absolutely nothing to gain from it. It is as though whatever is happening is not to their liking, and they'll make *sure* that no good will come of it. Their approach is less than healthy, not very practical, and certainly not an intelligent way to look at the problem.

The way they are reacting to the change is almost entirely the result of the programming they have received. Some people, because of their programming, see themselves as being optimistic and positive and ready to make the best of any situation. Other people, also because of their programming, see the world as being against them. The people in this second group gain the *least* from *anything* that happens to them.

Assuming that you are in the first group of people—those who look for the good instead of the bad—if you were to make a list right now of the possible gains that you could create from any change that's happening in your life, *how long would your list be?* The length of your list will determine, in part, how successful you will be in dealing with *any* change you encounter.

Your rule should be: Make sure that your list of things that you could *gain* from this change is longer than your list of things that you could *lose*.

8. What are the *other* changes that are brought on by *this* change?

If you're dealing with the change, first figure out the primary change you're dealing with, and name it. Next, make a mental list of the other changes that will come as a result of it: *loss, separation, direction,* etc. The purpose of learning to recognize each of the messengers of change for what they really are is to give you more control in managing the situation.

If you are really aware of what is going on around you, you give yourself a better chance of taking care of what is going on inside of you. Learning to recognize all of the messengers of change doesn't take time; i' just takes giving it a little thought.

9. Who else is affected by this change?

When you go through a change, you often become the messenger of change in the lives of the people around you. It is not our responsibility to live other people's lives for them. But the more you understand the changes you're helping to create in *their* lives, and the more empathy you have for their situation, the more maturity you will bring to your own process of changing.

You cannot function as a "mature" individual without first taking personal responsibility for your own actions. And a vital part of personal responsibility is recognizing the effects that *your* changes—and the way you deal with those changes—have on the lives of people around you. Having empathy for those important people in your life means that you understand what they are going through as a result of the changes that *you* are going through—and that you care.

You cannot help but get better at dealing with changes of your own if you practice helping others understand and deal with the changes in their lives. Beyond that is the fact that when you deal with other people in a sensible and sensitive way, you build more self-esteem.

Being aware of what others are going through when they face the same kinds of changes that you do, helps you in another way. It lets you really appreciate that you're not alone, that whatever it is you are facing, almost everyone else has already gone through it or one day will. It helps to know you're not in this by yourself.

10. What are the effects this change is having on you?

Whatever the change, ask yourself the question "Am I dealing with it well?" Do you like what's going on? Are you noticing other changes? How about your life right now—is it in turmoil? Is it confusing, or are things pretty well under control? Is the change affecting your relationship with anyone else? Are you happy to be here right now, or do you wish the change would just stop or go away? Do you look forward to more of the same? Do you feel like you're on top of things? If you could go back and do it over, would you do it the same way again?

Answering the question about the effects the change is having on you is like giving yourself a quick checkup. While you are going through any important change, it is *essential* that you take care of yourself.

You are important, and you deserve to have the best self-care that you can get. So look in on yourself now and then; find out how you're doing. How are you feeling? How is your health? Is the change bringing on a lot of stress? If the change weren't taking place right now, what other effects would *not* be happening in your life?

It is the effects that the change is having on *you* that can make this change a success or a failure. We're going to learn later just how powerful a role these personal effects of change play in the process of learning to excel. The change itself is not the most important issue; what happens to you and inside of you *is!*

11. What are you really afraid of?

Problems create fear. You may give fear a dozen other names, but when you strip life down to the bare essentials of psychological motivation in human beings, you will find that no matter how well-disguised it is, when you are dealing with problems, you are dealing with fear.

Here is an exercise that will help make this clear. It is an exercise that you may also want to mark for later reference. Ask yourself the following questions, and in your mind or on paper, fill in the answers:

WHAT AM I AFRAID OF?

1. Do I have a problem (yes or no)? _____
2. What is the real problem? _____
3. What bothers me about this problem? _____
4. What am I actually afraid of? _____
5. Is this fear real or imagined? _____
6. What can I do to deal with this fear? _____

It can be very healthy just to say the words "What I am afraid of is _____" and finish the sentence for yourself. Remember that most of our fears are deeply rooted in the long-forgotten mental programs of our childhood. What was programmed into our young computer-like brains way back then may have been covered over with layer after layer of other programs that hide the faces of our fears from us. But even though they are hidden, they are still there, and they are very powerful.

What we easily forget is that there is nothing wrong with having those fears. They are normal. They are a part of everyone's life. But we tend to hide them, pretending we are brave and telling ourselves all is well, even when we feel the clutching in our stomach that tries to tell us that all is not well, and we are afraid.

When you are learning to excel during a time of change, it is usually safer to look at the fear and recognize it for what it is. It is then that you can deal with the fear and put it in its proper place. But if you don't know what's driving you, it's hard to know what to do about it. When you feel the tension way down inside, and you sense the anxiety that is there, ask yourself the question "What am I afraid of?"

Don't just say—as a seven-year-old might—"I'm not afraid of *anything!*" Recognize the fear, get it out in the open, and face it. If you feel you need help doing that, there are excellent counselors who are trained to help you. But however you proceed to conquer the fear, when you confront it, you'll feel better about yourself, and you'll make dealing with the change itself easier.

12. How strongly is this change affected by the emotions involved?

If there are strong emotions involved, whose emotions are they? Are they yours, mostly yours, or mostly someone else's? Can you still look at the situation clearly in spite of the emotions, or are your feelings getting in the way of clear thinking?

I know it doesn't always help when you are in the middle of the change, and going through strong emotions, to try to sit down and calmly ask yourself "How much of what I'm going through is caused by my emotions (or by somebody else's)?" But in a quieter moment, during a less emotional time, it is important to ask yourself this question, give yourself the answer, and decide what you're going to do about it.

If you were using the help of a counselor or a therapist to get you through the problem, that therapist would walk you through the exact same process. If you want to figure out what to do next, you have to know where you stand. To find out where you stand, you have to find out how much emotion you're dealing with.

Knowing that the emotion is there will probably *not* take the emotion away. It may lessen it a little for a while, but it is the change you are going through that is creating the biochemical changes in the brain that are causing you to manifest the emotions you are feeling. You can have some control over those emotions by controlling some of the programs that you're giving to yourself—what you choose to think about, what you choose to tell yourself. But the key is to keep yourself clearly aware of the role that emotions—especially *your* emotions—are playing in the change that you're going through. You then give yourself at least a *chance* of dealing with them.

13. Is this a change that you wanted to happen?

This question should be asked two or three times at two or three different levels. I'll give you an example.

Let's say that Margaret has worked for Leonard for seven years. She has generally gotten along fairly well with Leonard, but she has also often told herself that she was going to quit. She doesn't like some of the ways that Leonard does business, and she especially doesn't like the way Leonard treats most of his employees. But Margaret's job pays well, she has gotten a few promotions over the seven years, and she usually tells herself that she plans to work for the same company as long as they'll have her.

Then something happens, and Leonard and Margaret have a fight. The relationship that they have developed over the years has been strained, and it could break. But Leonard now relies on Margaret, and Margaret now relies on Leonard—and on her job. So it comes to the point that both of them have to look at the relationship and decide if it should continue. The fourth messenger of change, *relationship*, visits Margaret, and Margaret begins to see that a major change is about to happen; she may be about to change her professional relationship with her boss.

At first she is upset, and, of course, she is concerned about her future. But let's say that the messenger of change asks Margaret the question "Is this a change that you wanted to happen?"

Margaret's first response is "No. I need my job, and I want it to continue." Then she is asked the same question again, and this time Margaret answers, "I've gotten along well with Leonard for seven years; it's been a good working relationship, and I would hate to see it end now."

But then she is asked the same question once again: *"Is this a change that you wanted to happen?"* and this time Margaret really *thinks* about her answer.

She thinks about what has worked, and she thinks about what hasn't. She lets herself see a clearer picture of the progress she has made during the seven years, not only professionally, but personally, within herself. Margaret thinks about her attitudes in dealing with people, and the different attitudes that seem to come from her boss.

And instead of just thinking about what she might lose if her job comes to an end now, Margaret begins to think about what she might *gain*. She begins to see the future, and to look at it differently from the way she has for the past seven years. Finally, after giving the matter a lot of thought, Margaret answers the question for the *third* time—and this time she says, "I didn't realize it, but way down deep, *this is a change that I wanted to happen.*"

There are those who say that we consciously (or unconsciously) create *all* of the changes that take place in our lives. I'm not sure that's true for all changes, but I do suspect that what we want—what we *really* want—is responsible for creating many of the changes that we go through.

14. What result do you want to avoid?

When you're dealing with a change, and you ask yourself the question "What result do I want to avoid?" it is not a negative way to look at the situation—you're just being practical. What would you like *not* to have happen?

That's a fair question, and one that can help you stop problems before they arise. If you know very clearly in your own mind what you want to avoid as a result of the change, you will set yourself up to watch out for it. It is a way of sensitizing yourself to be aware of the possibilities. Just as a soldier on maneuvers is constantly alert for signs of the enemy, it is common sense for us to be alert and to be on the lookout for anything that could work against us.

The problem with this approach is that many people carry it too far. They don't try to, but their own past negative programming automatically sets them up to see the worst first and the best last. The result of that is that some people are always looking for the bad news and never looking for the good.

When you ask yourself the question "What would I like *not* to have happen?" be cautious, clearly look at what you do not want to take place, and adjust your plan accordingly. The next question will help you do that.

15. What result do you want to create?

I recommend that you think about this question more than any other. When you think about what you really want to create—what you choose to have happen as a result of the change you're going through—you are giving yourself strong mental programs—images and messages that you feed to your own brain—that tell your mental computer what to seek and find.

The brain is designed to take action on the strongest programs it holds. So give it strong programs. Tell your own computer-brain what you want it to do; show it pictures; see the results over and over that you expect to create. See yourself having already accomplished the goal. The more you do that, the more you will change *chance* to *determination*, and the more you will change your *objectives* into *action*.

That, of course, is the basis of all positive self-programming techniques. But it all has to start with your knowing the result that you want to create.

16. What is one thing you could do right now to make this change work better for you?

What can you do today to make the change you are working on more positive? Can you learn something more about it? Can you improve your situation by taking some specific action? Would it help to write out a short list of personal goals that would help you clarify where you stand?

A strong personal decision to make things work is vital to dealing with change successfully. You may reach the conclusion that for the moment you should do absolutely nothing at all. But even coming to that conclusion is doing *something* to deal with the change more effectively.

The key is making a choice to do something. Making that choice of action puts you more in control.

17. Are you listening to the opinions of others, or are you listening to yourself?

The most important of all the opinions you hear is your own. If you want an opinion from someone else, ask for it. If you don't want an opinion, make the decision to keep your own counsel.

But in any change you're dealing with, ask yourself the question "Am I being influenced by someone else?" If you are, put that influence and that person to the test in your mind. If the influence or the opinion could in any way be working against you, does that person have the *right* to be forcing his or her opinions on you? Or are you *allowing* the opinions to come in because you have failed to know your own mind and take a strong stand for yourself?

This, too, is a matter of taking personal responsibility. If you are allowing someone else to make your choices for you by the force of their opinions, you are giving control of your life ultimately to someone else.

18. If you were asked to rate (from 1 to 10) the level of self-confidence you have in dealing with this change, how would you rate yourself?

Look at yourself in the mirror and ask yourself the question "*How am I doing?*" Give yourself a mental inspection and a report card. Evaluate your progress by giving yourself a situation report.

All successful organizations take the time to evaluate what has happened in the past, determine where they stand now, and reassess the future. If we want to be successful, we, as individuals, should not be any different. It can be a positive and uplifting experience to ask yourself to rate your own level of self-confidence in dealing with any change that you're going through.

Ask yourself how well you're doing. I hope that as we move on and explore the process of how to make the most of change, your answer to the question "How well am I doing?" will be *"Better and better."*

19. What—if anything—is working against you in dealing with this change?

Sometimes there *are* outside forces working against you in a change. You may not be able to do anything to get rid of the opposition—but look for it and be aware if it is there.

Look for opposition you *can* do something about. Consider whether or not the *something* that is working against you could be *you yourself.* This is another good opportunity to ask yourself the question "How is my attitude?" Ask yourself whether *you* are doing anything that could be getting in your own way.

If it is one of your own habits, your personal style or your own attitude that is working against you, you may figure it out, but you may not find the solution an easy one to put into practice. If you ever fall into the trap of thinking *"That's just the way I am, and there's nothing I can do about it,"* let me assure you that if you really want to get out of your own way, *you can.*

To do that takes some reprogramming—some decisive changes in your own Self-Talk, in what you tell yourself you want and expect from you. I won't suggest that getting out of your own way is something you can do by making a simple choice to do so one day and have it happen the next. You are dealing with years of programming that taught you to be the way you are. You've had a lot of practice doing it one way, but one good solution is to begin practicing doing things a *different* way.

A good place to start is with your own Self-Talk. For the next few weeks, try saying this to yourself every hour on the hour. *"I never get in my own way; I choose not to be a part of the problem. I choose to make things work."*

Along with practicing the new Self-Talk, make the decision to practice doing nothing that gets in your way—and start now. Practice doing and thinking things that always work for you instead of against you. The key to successfully managing your own position and role in dealing with change is *Self-Talk* and *practice*.

20. Are you ready to deal with this change?

This is one of those important questions that sound so simple. And yet, the answer to this question can tell you what you need to do next. If you ask yourself the question and find that your answer is "No—I am not ready to deal with this change," you alert yourself to the need to *get prepared.*

If your answer is "Yes—I am ready to deal with this change," you alert yourself to the chance to find the potential opportunities that the change might bring.

The next time you deal with any important change in your life, ask yourself the question "Am I ready to deal with this change?" The answer you give yourself will signal what you need to do next.

■

■ PERSONAL EXERCISE ■

Make an inventory of your assets for dealing with change.

How many times in the past in dealing with a major change in your life have you sat down and made a list of your assets? It is not something that we were trained to do. And yet, most truly successful people consistently recognize and list their assets. If you don't know what you've got going for you, how can you possibly know how strong you are?

On the following sample list, check one of the boxes after each asset. Rate each asset as being low, medium, or high (strong) as it relates to you now.

A List of My Assets

	Low	Medium	High
1. My courage	____	____	____
2. My conviction	____	____	____
3. My education	____	____	____
4. My experience	____	____	____
5. My perspective	____	____	____
6. My supportive friends	____	____	____
7. My determination	____	____	____
8. My attitude	____	____	____
9. My goals	____	____	____
10. My self-esteem	____	____	____
11. My self-belief	____	____	____
12. My sense of humor	____	____	____
13. My willingness to try	____	____	____
14. My thorough understanding of the problem	____	____	____

	Low	Medium	High
15. My plan	_____	_____	_____
16. My timetable	_____	_____	_____
17. Knowing what I want	_____	_____	_____
18. My willingness to risk	_____	_____	_____
19. Enjoying the challenge	_____	_____	_____
20. My willingness to see it through and make it work	_____	_____	_____

Plan to review this evaluation in 90 days and in 120 days from now. Are any of your assets changing as you practice working on them? (That is one of the objectives for completing this exercise and reviewing it again later.) Take the time to think about your assets and evaluate each of them.

Recognize your assets and use them.

The list of obstacles that actually stand in your way will never be as long as the list of assets you already have.

14

The Six Key Steps for Dealing with Change

There are six steps that will help you manage almost any personal change better. These steps are not difficult to follow, but they take some practice and some getting used to. The first three steps help you *understand* the change and how you *feel* about it. The second three steps help you decide what to *do* about the change. The six steps are:

1. Recognize and understand the change
2. Accept or reject the change
3. Choose your attitude
4. Choose your style
5. Choose your action
6. Review, evaluate, and adjust

Let's learn to use these six steps and how to apply each of them to specific situations in your own life.

▪ | *Step 1—Recognize and Understand the Change*

The first step is to openly recognize—and understand—the *specific* change you're dealing with. If you see a change that could affect you in any way, learn everything you can about it. Focus on it. Give it some real attention; think about it, and figure it out. The more you know about the change, the better you will be able to deal with it. In order to see the change clearly and understand it for what it really is, begin by asking yourself the questions in Chapter 16, and seriously thinking through your answers.

This is the first step in taking the changes in your life out of the hands of chance. The more you know about the change, the more you will give yourself the opportunity to be in control of the change—or you will at least give yourself the chance to have as much control in the matter as you can.

The changes that seem to bother us most are the changes that we feel we have no control over. It is as though the world is leading us instead of us being in charge of our own lives.

A lot of what I have written in the past has been about taking responsibility for ourselves. And it is certainly true that if you want to have any measure of personal responsibility in your life, taking the responsibility to be in control of the changes that happen to you (or because of you) is one of the most important steps you can take.

But the place to start is *recognizing* the change and understanding it. One of the reasons that so many people feel so lost or overwhelmed by the massive social and cultural changes that are taking place all around us is that they fail to put this one step into action; they don't stop and think about what's going on long enough to recognize what is happening and how they feel about it. It's not that it's a difficult step; it's that no one taught us to do it, so we didn't get the practice.

Recognizing and understanding change doesn't come naturally to us, so for the next week or two, do this: Look at any change that you're going through right now, or any change you are aware of that is coming. Think it through. Ask yourself the questions that were just outlined, and give yourself clear, simple answers. You might be surprised at finding how crystal-clear those changes (and what they mean to you) start to become just by going through this one simple exercise.

Think about *any* change that is happening right now or that you believe is *about to* happen in your life, and ask yourself the question "What could I do if I really wanted to recognize and understand *everything* about this change?" Then go through the earlier list of questions and give yourself the answers. If you conscientiously undertake that one basic exercise, you will be doing something that most people never do. I have already pointed out that that isn't really their fault—we weren't taught to think about change in that way. But once we understand, we have an exceptionally effective new tool to use.

■

■ PERSONAL EXERCISES ■

1. Select a specific change that you want to manage successfully, and define every important element of the change—in detail—with a friend, or to yourself. Use the questions in Chapter 16 as an outline for your discussion.

2. Write out one- or two-word phrases to complete each of the following statements:

  a. The specific change I wish to manage successfully is:

    _____

  b. The cause of this change is:

    _____

  c. The principal obstacle to deal with is:

    _____

  d. The other people who are directing this change are:

    _____

  e. The opportunity that this change offers me is:

    _____

  f. The desired result of this change is:

    _____

  g. What I do not know about this change that I should know is:

    _____

  h. What I dislike most about this change is:

    _____

  i. What I like most about this change is:

    _____

  j. My overall level of understanding about this change is:

    _____

15

Step 2—Accept or Reject the Change

Is this a change you want to go along with, or would you like to have nothing to do with it?

When I am talking with individuals who are dealing with a new change, their first answer to that question is almost always that they don't have any choice. Then they think about it. If they think about it long enough, they usually begin to modify their position a little. "Maybe I do have a choice about this; maybe it *is* up to me to accept or reject this change."

Your best and most accurate starting point is to always assume that you might have *some* say-so in the matter. That doesn't sound like a workable position to take when something suddenly happens *to* you and it appears you can do absolutely nothing about it. But your decision to accept the change or reject it, or take some position between the two, will affect what you do next. You may not want to accept the fact that your invalid in-law is about to become a part of your family and you may have a lot of caretaking to do, but the option you have is almost *never* simply yes or no. We almost always have a few workable alternatives available to us if we take the time to think the problem through.

The question here is not just whether you will accept the change or not; the real issue is whether you will let the change, whatever it is, affect you in a positive or in an adverse way. No matter what the change, it is *always* up to you to accept dealing with it or reject dealing with it. So we're not talking here about denying the change when things don't go your way; we're working instead with your *acceptance* or *refusal* to either allow the change to happen, or to allow the change to affect you in a negative way.

Some people quietly go along with almost everything that happens to them, as though they had no control or no voice in the matter at all. Other people want to be in charge of *everything*, even when they can't be. A reasonable middle ground is the most sensible position to take when it comes to dealing with change. The rule might be: *"Don't give in unless you want to give in. Don't waste your time and your life fighting the changes you cannot stop. But always take the time to choose."*

When it comes to accepting or rejecting a change of any kind, perhaps the two most important Self-Talk statements, or *choices*, that you could make are:

"I choose to accept this change and to make it work."

"I do not accept this change, and I choose to find a way to *change the change* or rise above it."

Even when you think you have no choice, the truth is you almost always do. We have the right to say *"yes"* and to say *"no."* If you know what you want, and if you know what changes you choose to reject or accept, then you will be giving yourself the advantage.

■

■   **PERSONAL EXERCISES**   ■

Ask yourself the following questions about a change that you're working with now, or about a change you expect to face in the near future.

1. *On a scale of 1 to 10 (with 1 being not important at all, and 10 being most important), how important is this change?* _____

2. *Do I accept this change?* _____ *Why?* _____

3. *Do I reject this change?* _____ *Why?* _____

4. *Is this what I wanted to have happen?* _____

5. *If not, what did I want to happen instead?*

6. *If this isn't what I wanted to happen, is there anything now that I can do about it?* _____

7. *What can I do now to make this change more acceptable to me?*

16

Step 3—Choose Your Attitude

Your attitude—how you *feel* about the change—is *always* up to *you*! No one else has the right to determine *your* attitude about anything for you.

How you look at life and how you feel about yourself is entirely up to the attitude that you have. How you feel about the change will affect everything that you think about it and do about it. And there is no more important step you can take to deal with any change in its most positive way than choosing your attitude about the change.

In the previous two steps you recognized and understood the change, and then you made the choice to accept or reject it. Your choice now is to choose your attitude about what's happening, and the choice you make will affect, influence, and determine *everything* that you think and do about the change.

In the simplest terms, three of the most common attitudes are *positive*, *negative*, and *indifferent*. If you choose to have an optimistic attitude about the change, then you obviously need no encouragement to do so. If you choose to have a negative attitude about the change, then I would suggest that you reconsider. If you choose to have an attitude of indifference, I would ask you to go back through the two previous steps in Chapters 14 and 15, review them, and consider the importance—and the effect—that your attitude is about to have.

One of the most unknown, unrecognized, and un-used tools of the human mind is the recognition that *attitude* is always a *choice*. You can, right now, even while you're reading this, choose to feel happy about something—or unhappy. You can choose to give yourself the self-directions that motivate you to go for the good, or you can sit back and only wish that things would get better. You can create enthusiasm, excitement, anticipation, and the feeling of well-being, or you can sit back and wait for something else to push or move you.

Entire books have been written about the single subject of attitude. Enthusiastic inspirational speakers hold seminars throughout the nation, designed for the single purpose of elevating attitudes, and counselors and therapists spend hours enlightening and encouraging their clients for the same purpose. They do this because they recognize that *attitude is always a choice*!

Right now take a moment to think of a change that you are dealing with (or are about to face). Next, tell yourself the words "*I have a good attitude about this!*" Then lift your head just a little higher, and see yourself, in your own mind, meeting the challenge. Next, *smile*.

Go ahead, smile! Lift your head up, put your shoulders back, take a good, long, deep breath—and smile. When you hold your head up, hold it up high. When you put your shoulders back, let yourself feel the muscles stretch and the shoulders rise. And then look into the distance, *believe* in yourself, and *smile*.

Most people have no idea how much control they have over their own attitudes. What a powerful tool we have—simply by managing the computer input to the chemical control centers of our own brain—and we can put it to work anytime we want.

The biographies of successful people are filled with examples of how individuals overcame impossible odds, achieved impossible results, and took control of their own destinies by the simple act of taking control of their own *attitudes*. If you, right now or at any time, chose to do the same, there is no telling what you could do. It is true; when you choose to take control over your own attitude, give it energy, give it *life*, and put it to work, you can turn an experience from being *impossible*—to becoming an *achievement*.

The self-esteem, the self-respect, the self-confidence, and the self-belief that that one simple choice—to change your attitude—brings cannot even be measured.

Your choice to choose your attitude is more powerful than any other tool you will find to help make your life work. If you haven't tried it before, try it now. If you are used to selecting your attitude and using it to help you make things work, then when it comes to facing change, use it more than ever before. More kingdoms, more goals, more riches, and more happiness have been won or lost because of attitude than any other human characteristic.

Your attitude is one of the few assets you will ever have that is entirely yours to do with what you will. Choose your attitude, and you will choose how well change—and your future—is going to work for you.

■

■ **PERSONAL EXERCISES** ■

1. *Get a clear picture in your mind right now of the change you want to think about. Then complete the sentence:* "The change I am thinking about is: _____."

2. *Once you have a picture of that change clearly framed in your mind, ask yourself the following questions:*
    a. *What is my attitude about _____?* (*Repeat the name of the change to yourself.*)
    b. *How do I feel about this change?*
    _____

    c. *Why do I feel the way I do about this change?*
    _____

    d. *Are these my real feelings, or is this the way I think I'm supposed to feel?* _____
    e. *If I could choose to have any attitude that I wanted to have about this change, what would that attitude be?* _____
    f. *Since my attitude is always up to me, what attitude do I choose to have right now?* _____

3. *List three things you can do to create the strongest possible attitude for dealing with this change:*
    a. _____
    b. _____
    c. _____

_____

17

Step 4—Choose Your Style

Whatever the change is—how do you want to handle it? Do you want to go along with the change, develop a partnership with the change and work with it, passively resist it, actively resist the change, fight it, or actively support it?

With this step, you have another choice to make. If you were to outline your choices of style, they would look like this:

a. Acquiescence (or giving in) to the change
b. Partnership
c. Passive resistance
d. Active resistance
e. Full retreat
f. Active acceptance
g. Positive acceleration

These are the "styles" or the "methods" that people use when they deal with *any* change that takes place. These same styles are used by people whether the change is minor (decorating the family room) or major (getting a divorce, getting married, or changing a career path).

If you learn these seven basic operating styles of dealing with change, you will learn something about yourself—and the styles you have operated with in the past—and you will understand more about the operating styles of people around you.

At one time or another in our lives we all adopt one or more of these operating styles. Based on the nature of the change and our desire to have the change enter our lives, we may at any time adopt different styles. But over a period of years, most people will tend to adopt one style more than others. People who know about these styles usually have an edge. They are able to adopt one style or another *by choice*—and once again that puts them more in control of the changes they are dealing with. So you can adopt any style you *choose* to adopt.

Each of the styles has its own effect or result. As we go through the types of styles, be aware of which of these styles you have used or are currently using.

Style 1—Acquiescence (Giving In)

This is not necessarily a negative style, but it is not typically a style of strength. At times a strong person will use this style and "give in," but when a strong person gives in, it is usually a negotiating tool to gain something else.

Acquiescence means that you go along with the change. You don't fight it. You accept it and make the best of it. You don't have to like it, but you feel you can do nothing about it.

The problem with acquiescence as a style of dealing with change is that it is the "norm" for a lot of people. So much change is happening, there is so much going on, people feel there is nothing they can do about *anything*—and "giving in" to the change becomes a way of life. That not only makes acquiescence a questionable style; that's the opposite of taking control of your own life.

So you have to be careful about automatically acquiescing to change. Give in only when that is the most sensible thing to do. Give in to change when it is clear that there are no better alternatives. Give in when you have to do so to gain some time to think about what you should do next. And finally, give in to change when you recognize that nothing you can think of or say or do could possibly *stop* the change or *change* the change.

If you are in a relationship, and the other person makes a choice for his or her own reasons, and there is nothing appropriate for you to do to change his or her choice, you may have to accept it. If your company closes the division that you're working in, and you're suddenly out of work or in a different position, there may be nothing you can do about that. If the county decides to build a highway that takes up twenty feet of your front lawn, and there is nothing more you can do to stop the bulldozers but to stand in front of them, it is probably the time to acquiesce.

I have met some people who refuse to give in or give up regardless of the circumstances. Some of them

I respect; yet, with others I have to question their recognition of what truly is important in life and what is not. The old man, Harry Truman (not the president), who chose to stay on the mountainside of Mount Saint Helens when it was known that the mountain was about to explode and the volcano within it was about to destroy everything for miles around it, was one of those who chose not to give in. He refused to leave the mountain that he called his home. When Mount Saint Helens erupted, Harry Truman was buried in an avalanche of rocks and ash.

Instead of recognizing the possible value in acquiescence, Harry Truman fought for his life-style and his point of view. If one of Harry's goals was to live a little longer (which it apparently wasn't), he chose the wrong style for dealing with the change.

A woman named Ida Jean wanted more than anything in the world to become a registered nurse. Her husband had a career of his own, and in the process of following his career, he created changes in his and Ida Jean's home life that made her goal almost impossible to reach. But Ida Jean was intelligent. She thought it through. Instead of fighting the changes that took her away from reaching her goal of becoming an R.N., she acquiesced—she gave in.

But she gave in for a reason. She was patient, and she waited. In time, the opportunity to go back to school came up again—and this time she achieved the goal. If she had fought it and disrupted her family's life because of it, she might never have found the opportunity in front of her to go back to school. Ida Jean ended up not only becoming an R.N. and working in her chosen field, she went on to get an additional degree in the field of medicine. She "acquiesced," or gave in, for a time, but she had a plan. And in her case her chosen style of acquiescence worked.

Another woman named Rose wanted more than anything in the world to be a concert organist. She had studied piano and organ and she played beautifully. But because of her family life and her responsibilities as a mother—and because of the attitude of her family— she put her career aside and, instead of playing the organ, Rose played the mother.

I knew Rose when she was middle-aged, and I knew her later, when her family had left home and all that was left of her life was her marriage, her role as a mother, and her role as a wife. She had acquiesced. She had given in. She had accepted the change from concert organist to consummate housewife—and she had never achieved her goal.

You probably know someone who, like Ida Jean, gave in and lived with the change and made things work. You can probably think of other people who, like Rose, lost because they gave up too soon. When you see the loss, when you recognize the potential that individual could have reached—or when you observe what someone else *did* because he or she was patient and acquiesced for a time—you can clearly see the benefits—and the detriments of choosing the style of acquiescence.

Style 2—Partnership

This is the style that many business people use; they are taught the effectiveness of the partnership style of dealing with change, from their first year in business school to the day they retire. This is also the style that politicians and people in the public eye often use.

Partnership is like agreeing to a compromise with the change. This is the method of dealing with change that says "I'll go along with this, but let's work *together* on it." The key word here is *compromise*. This is different from acquiescence—you're not "giving in and giving up." You are simply recognizing that you can deal with this change better by making a "deal" with it. It is as though you are saying "Okay, I'll put up with this, I'll make the investment, but here's what I expect to get in return."

As an example of the partnership style, let's look at a man named Bob. Bob doesn't really want to attend night classes for nine weeks, but he has to in order to maintain his broker's license. Attending the classes is going to put a strain on his home life, and it will take some hard work and adjustment to get through it. So Bob says, "I'll live with this—I'll make the compromise—but I'm also going to make sure that I see the reward in front of me, and make sure that I get it."

In so doing, Bob creates a "partnership" with the change. He lives with it, he doesn't fight it, he determines what dealing with the change successfully will do for him, and he commits to it.

Forming a partnership with change is a style many people use without being aware of it. But there is a definite advantage in knowing what's going on. When you consciously consider what you are doing, you put yourself in more control, and you have a clearer picture of the objective and of what contribution you have to make.

By being aware of using the style of partnership, you give yourself a much better opportunity to weigh the costs against the benefits. If you say "I *choose* to use the style of partnership with this change," you immediately give yourself more control, and a greater advantage.

When you choose to use this style, you may not always get everything you want, but you will usually maintain at least partial control of the situation. The partnership style is usually safe, usually effective, and can be a positive way to deal with change.

Style 3—Passive Resistance

Passive resistance is a style that usually works only if you are very patient and you have a long time to work at getting what you want. The typical result of passive resistance is that you appear to go along with the change but underneath you are fighting it. You really don't like the change, and you don't intend to support it.

The wife who is operating in a mode of passive resistance says she approves of the move to the new city, but meanwhile she burns the toast. Things aren't to her liking, and her disapproval shows itself in subtle ways.

The man who disagrees silently with his wife's new career as a paralegal in a law office somehow plans the vacation to directly conflict with the seminar that his wife has to attend.

The young lady who is about to walk down the aisle with a man she is not quite sure she really wants to marry suddenly becomes ill—and all the plans and even the marriage itself must be put off. She is showing every sign of dealing with the problem by using passive resistance.

This is a style of dealing with change that most people adopt unconsciously. And the style of passive resistance is used every day by people who would do almost anything to avoid the change they are expected to make.

A few people with high self-esteem can use this style to their benefit, knowing full well what they're doing. They are the exception.

The lesson in learning about passive resistance is to recognize that it almost never works. It represents a lack of personal control; it underscores a sense of the lack of personal responsibility. And when used, the style of passive resistance almost never builds self-esteem. If you are dealing with a change in your life that you would rather not support or go along with, one of the *other* styles of dealing with change is almost always a better choice than the style of passive resistance.

Style 4—Active Resistance

This style, though it has its consequences, can often be a positive style of dealing with change. If you are actively resisting the change, you are at least aware of how you feel about the change and what you want to do about it.

This is when your employer tells you the company is starting a general layoff of employees at your level, and you choose to fight the change—at least when it comes to you—because you have more to offer. This is when you hear the statistics of an economic downturn reported on television telling you that jobs in your field are about to become scarce or harder to get—and you refuse to let the statistics keep you from getting a better job.

This is when you are told by the church council that the youth program has to be shut down because there isn't enough money being contributed to keep it running, and you decide to keep it running. Active resistance is when you decide to openly fight the change.

With things changing the way they are these days, it would not make any sense at all to resist every change that is happening. But it makes a great deal of sense to resist the changes in your own personal life that could harm you or hold you back, and to support the changes that will help you excel.

Style 5—Full Retreat

Another style of dealing with change is to avoid it completely—and with some of the changes that confront us, that may not be a bad idea. If you don't *like* the change, nothing says that you have to sit down at the negotiating table and make friends with it. Some changes should never be admitted into your life at all.

A good example of this would be your decision to not spend time with someone who, contrary to your wishes, wants to spend time with you. Let's say that the other person wants to be close to you, and wants to establish a strong relationship with you. So you go through the steps of dealing with change: You recognize and understand the potential change and what it would mean to your personal life; you make the conscious choice to reject the change; you then choose your attitude (in this case, you decide to be positive about your next move), and your next move is—by *your choice*—a full tactical retreat.

As you can see, a full retreat doesn't necessarily mean that you are *running* from the situation. It simply means that you choose to depart from it.

Style 6—Active Acceptance

This style is easy, and it is almost always positive. When you make the choice to use active acceptance as your style for dealing with change, you are telling yourself, "I'm going along with this; I'm going to help make this work."

Let's say that you look in the mirror one morning and decide that it's time to lose some weight. You step on the scale, and that confirms it! Most people, when confronted by that situation, believe that what they're going to do next is called a diet. And so they face the prospect of dieting to lose weight. But you know that what you're really facing is a significant *change* in your habits and attitudes for the next weeks or months.

Instead of thinking "I guess I'd better go on a diet," you sit down for a few minutes and go over your list of steps for dealing with change. First, you recognize and understand the change that you are asking of yourself. You think about it, and you really come to grips with every aspect of the challenge in front of you.

In this case, let's say that you decide to accept the change instead of rejecting it—you're going to go through with the diet. The next step you take is to choose your attitude. Let's say that you really need to lose the weight, and you've been wanting to go on a diet for a long time. You want to feel healthier; you want to look better, and you want to feel better about yourself. Your weight has been getting in the way of your self-esteem, and it's time to feel good again. So you make the choice to have a positive attitude about dieting, exercising, losing weight, feeling good, and liking yourself.

Next comes the step of choosing your style of dealing with the change. Instead of acquiescence, partnership, passive resistance, active resistance, or full retreat, as an operating style you consciously *choose* active acceptance. You're going to accept the changes in your life (both the sacrifices and the results) and *you are going to actively support your decision to lose the weight.*

This is an important step. Many people make the decision to lose the weight—and then they resent their own decision and fight it every minute they're on the diet. (No wonder it doesn't work!)

Choosing to use active acceptance as your style of dealing with change can even help when you are accepting a change that you don't want to accept. An example of this would be if it was the doctor who told you you needed to lose the weight instead of you making the decision for yourself. Now you know you *have to* go through the same process even if you don't really want to—but you also know that using the positive style of active acceptance can make an important difference in how well you do.

Active acceptance is nearly always a good choice of style to use when dealing with an important change—as long as the change is good for you—whether making the change is your choice or not.

Style 7—Positive Acceleration

Positive acceleration means that as a style of dealing with change, you choose to not just go along with it or make things okay—*you choose to give it everything you've got!* Instead of letting change happen *to* you, you start taking charge. You make the change work for you instead of against you in every way that you can.

Positive acceleration is the style of change that is

almost automatically adopted by the most "successful" people. By using positive acceleration in dealing with change, they not only get through it, they literally achieve more *because* of it.

Carl was a salesman who worked out of a small office in Wheaton, Illinois. His territory was the state of Illinois, and he had spent five years with his company building his territory to the point that he reached every income goal he set each sales quarter. Out of the blue, his company announced to Carl that they were changing his sales territory. He could keep his office in the Chicago area if he wanted to, but they were reassigning him to the state of Indiana.

The salesman who had previously handled Indiana had not worked very hard, and the territory wasn't well developed. So when Carl first heard the news, his first thought was rebellion: He decided to quit! (That would be adopting a style of full retreat.) But that had never been Carl's style, so the idea of quitting passed quickly, and he immediately began to revert to his normal style of dealing with change in an optimistic way.

I won't underestimate the amount of work Carl had to do in the next months, but the result of his style of positive acceleration was that Carl and the state of Indiana outstripped Illinois in sales, and Carl had turned a real problem into a triumph.

Carl could have just as easily chosen any other style of dealing with the change—and lost or failed because of it. And in the exact same way that Carl chose to make the change work for him instead of against him, you have the opportunity to select your style with every change you face.

■

■ PERSONAL EXERCISES ■

1. Complete the sentence.
   "In the past, I have been
   _____ a. generally unaware of the styles of dealing with change."
   _____ b. somewhat aware of, and using the styles of dealing with change, without really thinking about it."
   _____ c. actively and consciously choosing and implementing the styles of dealing with change in my life."

2. What is the style you use most frequently when dealing with key changes in your life?
   a. Acquiescence _____
   b. Partnership _____
   c. Passive resistance _____
   d. Active resistance _____
   e. Full retreat _____
   f. Active acceptance _____
   g. Positive acceleration _____

3. Complete the following sentence.
   "I believe that the style of dealing with change I most frequently use now
   _____ a. is working against me."
   _____ b. is not working for me as well as it could be."
   _____ c. on the average is working okay for me."
   _____ d. is working most of the time."
   _____ e. is helping me to excel."

4. Do you want to do anything to change your most frequently used style of dealing with change? Yes _____ No _____

5. Which personal style would you prefer to use most often in dealing with change? _____

6. List three reasons for wanting to improve your style of dealing with change, or practice using your chosen style more effectively.

    a. _____

    b. _____

    c. _____

18

Step 5—Choose
Your Action

One of the most important steps in any form of problem solving is also a key player in dealing with change. You'll find that when you put this step into play, you will not only be helping yourself deal with the change successfully, you will at the same time be working at solving problems the change has created.

The reason for going through the previous four steps in dealing with change is to get to this step. Learning to recognize and understand the change is important; it's essential. Making the decision to accept or reject the change is key. Choosing your attitude will affect how you feel about everything you think and do about the change. Choosing your style puts you in control of how you handle what happens next.

But more than any other step you take to deal with change effectively, *choosing your action* is ultimately what will make the change work for you or against you. In dealing with change, there is nothing more important than what you actually *do* about it.

If you go through the steps, you should begin to define at least your general course of action. Now it is time to get specific: What *action* do you take today? What action do you take tomorrow?

Some people are uncomfortable with the thought of having to analyze something. It is as though an analysis of the appropriate action is a complicated process. It isn't. The best analysis of this kind of situation always starts with asking yourself the right questions, and giving yourself straightforward answers. If you do that, your next course of action will begin to be laid out for you. You may not choose to do what the answers suggest to you, but at least you'll know, in your own best judgment, what you should do if you want to make the choice work for you.

■ | *Your Choice of "Style" and Your Choice of "Action" Should Work Together*

If, when you took the time to think the change through completely, you took the time to choose your style well, you should already have a good idea of the kind of action you will take. Your choice of style determines the style of action you take—or, at least, it should. That's not always the case, however. I've known people who have adopted a style that is strong and assertive, at least in their *minds*, but when it got down to taking action, they weren't as strong as they thought they'd be.

Sometimes this is caused by a situation that is intimidating. How you think you'll deal with it and how you actually deal with it can be two different things, because the situation seems somehow "bigger than you are." But another reason that people's actions sometimes fail to follow their better judgment is that they haven't taken the time to specifically determine the course of action they should be taking.

If you think you ought to be doing *something*, and you're determined to take some action and gain control of the situation but aren't sure exactly what to do, you may end up doing no more than making a big fanfare and doing very little. We are told that our cave-dwelling ancestors did a lot of that. When a neighboring tribe got too close, or when a thunderstorm threatened, they were likely to jump up and down, do a lot of yelling, and throw sticks and rocks at the ground. I don't know if they actually did that, but having observed the antics of some of our more contemporary relatives, I have noticed a certain similarity.

■ What Is the Most Important Thing You *Can Do* Next?

There is a big difference between planning to take action and reaching the goal. The missing ingredient is usually the action step itself. Telling yourself "I really need to do something about this" isn't enough. Even the single most effective means of succeeding ever known—*being determined*—will do little more than help you become battered and bruised like someone who is flailing at windmills, if you haven't decided *specifically* what to do next.

Some people like to live on the edge and deal with life with no plan at all. They see life as a constant challenge, a duel between masters, a battle of wits in which the ultimate objective is not really the mastery of life—it is in the battle; it is in the game itself. To some, a strategy of well laid-out plans and action steps is for children or novices; they would rather "go it alone" and take their inspiration from surprise. But that would be like choosing your marriage partner by drawing a name from a hat. It puts you into partnership with luck, and leaves what happens next up to chance.

■ It's Still a Good Idea

The suggestion that you first decide what action steps you're going to take and then actually write them down and review them regularly is not new. All good goal-setting plans include this vital step. Deciding what to do—*and then writing it down*—is a singularly effective way to help yourself take the action you choose. It is a method of creating successes that is so well proven that by now it is self-evident: *write down, on paper, the steps you plan to take.*

But actually doing it takes *practice*—enough so that it becomes a habit. And that is where many people fall short. We weren't taught from our earliest days of childhood—once we learned how to print words on paper—to write goals, write plans, write down "action steps," review them every day, adjust them as necessary, and follow them. Some people learn those techniques in business, or from a self-improvement book. But most people never learn to actually practice using the techniques.

In this book you will have an opportunity to use those techniques for yourself. In Chapter 26, "Your Personal Book of Changes," you will find a step-by-step guide that takes you through this process and gives you the opportunity to "fill in the blanks," to help you outline for yourself the steps you may want to take in dealing with *any* change. At that time, practice writing out action steps. It's a great feeling to know that you're actually *doing something*; you're actually taking action—and working on the problem. It's an even greater feeling to know that you're back in charge, and you know where you're going.

■

■ **PERSONAL EXERCISES** ■

1. *Complete the sentence: "The change I am facing is*

_____

2. *Answer the following questions with regard to the change you are facing now:*
   a. *If you could do anything you wanted to do about this change, what would it be?* _____
   b. *What are the three best courses of action to take in dealing with this change?*

(1) _____

(2) _____

(3) _____

   c. *If you don't know what to do next, how can you find out?* _____
   d. *Are you willing to take the action you know you need to take?* _____
   e. *What will probably happen if you do not take action in dealing with this change?* _____
   _____
   f. *What will the most likely outcome be if you do take action?* _____
   _____
   _____

19

Step 6—Review, Evaluate, and Adjust

This step is perhaps the easiest of all the steps to perform—and perhaps that is why it is the easiest to overlook or ignore: *Review, evaluate,* and *adjust* as necessary.

Think of any change you're dealing with and review every step you are taking in dealing with it. Do you recognize and understand the change for what it really is and what it really means to you? Have you made a conscious choice that tells you for certain whether you accept or reject the change? Have you chosen your attitude—and are you living up to your choice? Is the style you've chosen working for you? If it is, can you use it to even better advantage? If your style isn't working as well as you'd like, is it time to try a different style? And is your action plan in place—are you taking action, and is it the *right* action?

I often think about the problems we, as individuals, could solve if we sat down once or twice a week as business people do—and had a meeting to review the problem. But most people—even those who have review meetings every day at the office—forget to apply the same sensible step to dealing with the *rest* of their lives.

Schedule a twenty-minute session with a friend (or with yourself) for the singular purpose of *reviewing* and *evaluating* the steps that are outlined in the previous chapters—and watch what happens! Many people are astounded at the results they create by attending to that one simple, final step. Schedule a time—regularly—and complete the process: review your progress, decide what adjustments you need to make, follow through, watch your results, and schedule your next review.

■ A Good Way to Get Started

If you have followed each step of the process of dealing with change so far, and if you have used it to deal with a specific change, you should, by this time, be thinking about taking *personal control* in dealing with that change. That is our one underlying objective in this entire process: *to give you more personal control.*

Even if you have not yet isolated a specific change or problem that you're dealing with right now, and have not applied each one of the steps to something that is taking place in your life today, the six steps themselves (this step included) serve a second purpose.

Even by reading through these steps, we tend to

become more aware of the control that we actually do have.

Reading through Step #1 gives you the opportunity to question for yourself how much about the change you really know, and it underscores the fact that the more you know, the better chance you'll have of dealing with it. Every time you face a new change ask yourself the question *"Do I recognize that this is a change that's happening in my life, and how much do I know about it?"* If you asked yourself that question just once or twice a day, you may—within a matter of a few days—change how you deal with the problems or the opportunities that that change represents.

Similarly, knowing that you can consciously *choose* to accept the change or not accept the change may not change the change itself (it doesn't change what's happening right now), but knowing that you're in the process of *dealing* with the change begins to give you the assurance that you *do* have some choices in the matter.

And certainly, little more needs to be said about what happens when you choose to have a good *attitude* about something. It seems that this is one of those truths that we all recognize—some of us just never got into the habit of actually doing it. How often do you say to yourself "Right now, at this very moment, I'm going to choose the attitude I want to have?" Once again, this step takes almost no time at all, and yet its results are always worthwhile.

The same is true for your choice of style. It doesn't take long to make a decision for yourself about how you want to act and how you want to respond to something. Sometimes just reading, first thing in the morning, a written reminder that is taped to your mirror, is enough to get you thinking about your style and then taking action on it right then, that day. Actually choosing the style you will use to deal with any situation or any problem is a choice that is easy to forget to make. We weren't taught to think "What is my style?" or "What style do I choose to use about this?" so we have to remind ourselves.

When you are reviewing these six steps to evaluate your decisions and make sure you're doing the best thing that you can, choosing your action is a step that can take a little longer to consider. It's the one thing we seem to be least sure of. You may wonder, "Am I *really* doing the right thing?" But this, too, does not have to be a chore. Ask yourself the question *"Am I doing the right thing about this right now?"* or *"Is what I'm doing working?"* Or ask yourself *"Is there something else that I ought to be doing?"*

■ Ask Yourself the Questions

When you ask the right questions, you not only create the answers, but you also build your own conscious *awareness* of what you're doing. You're actually *doing something about your life,* and you know it!

And that builds experience, confidence, and self-esteem; that helps keep you on track and helps you win. People who never think about this process and never consider the changes they're going through most often are among the least successful people in dealing with change. On the other hand, people who are vitally aware of the changes that are going on in their lives and who are taking an active personal role in the results of those changes are always the most successful.

Doesn't it make sense, then, to say, *"From now on, I choose to be in control of every change in my life!"* Taking that position certainly won't change those things over which you have no personal control. But taking that position will almost always affect the results of those changes in a more positive way.

■

■ PERSONAL EXERCISES ■

Refer to the following list of steps and short script of positive Self-Talk each time you want to deal with a change more effectively. Make a photocopy of the steps and the following Self-Talk phrases and keep them where you can refer to them often.

The Six Steps for Dealing with Change

Step 1: "*I recognize and understand the change.*"

Step 2: "*I make the decision to accept or reject the change.*"

Step 3: "*I choose my attitude.*"

Step 4: "*I choose my style.*"

Step 5: "*I choose the action I take every day.*"

Step 6: "*I review these steps and evaluate my progress daily.*"

Your Personal Self-Talk for Dealing with Change

"*I always deal with change successfully.*"
"*I am good at making positive changes in my life.*"
"*I never leave the changes in my life up to chance or up to anyone else.*"
"*I enjoy taking responsibility for myself, and I always do.*"
"*I always deal with change in the most positive way.*"
"*I am good at dealing with change!*"

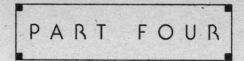

PART FOUR

The Change
in You

20

Changing Your Perception About Change

It should be apparent by now that there is a purpose for looking at change so closely. Throughout most of this book we have looked at changes as they relate directly to you. Now we go one step further. Now it is time to hold up the looking glass and learn what you see when you look at *yourself.*

Any change that takes place in your life is either a Change of Limitation—a change that hurts you or holds you back, or a Change of Progression—a change that helps you to achieve. With a little practice, you should be able to identify any change you or someone you know is dealing with, and determine which of these two categories that change fits into.

Our objective here is to learn to turn all changes into Changes of Progression—even those you thought were Changes of Limitation. The key to making changes work for you is to recognize that it is your own perspective that makes a change seem like a limitation.

For example, to one person, the change of relocation can be thought of as a catastrophe filled with nothing but problems, with no good to come of it. Someone else in exactly the same circumstance, making the same kind of move, can see the same change as filled with *opportunity* and *potential*, and can't wait to get on with it.

One person will fight a required change in jobs, while another person in similar circumstances will see the same job change as a chance to do something different and to get out of the rut or move on. One person will see the end of a relationship as the end of the world; another person in the same kind of breakdown in a relationship will learn from it and grow because of it.

No two individuals and no two circumstances of change are exactly alike, of course. But most people tend to automatically regard the changes in their lives either as limitations or as opportunities.

Ask yourself the question *"Do I typically see changes in my life as Changes of Limitation, or do I see them as Changes of Progression?"* In asking yourself that question, you are asking yourself something that is at the heart of your present ability to excel. What you are saying is "Do I let changes limit me? Or do I choose to always make the changes in my life work *for* me?"

What is your first reaction when loss, separation, relocation, changes in relationships, a change in direction, or a change in health occurs? Do you most easily see those changes as trouble or bothersome or something that could get in your way? Or do you have the perspective to always see the best side of it and look forward to making the most of it?

■ The Difference Between "Attitude" and "Perception"

Changing your "perception" about change is broader and more encompassing than choosing your "attitude" about change. One is the feeling you have (attitude) about the change; the other is the picture you have, the mental hold and assessment (perception) that you have of the change. Your choice of attitude will help you determine your feelings about the change—but your perception deals with your understanding and comprehension.

The closer you look at the change and the more clearly you can see the facts involved, the more awareness you'll have of what you're actually dealing with. It is that closer look, that clearer assessment, that can give you the insight to find the means to turn the situation from a Change of Limitation to a Change of Progression.

Imagine that you are walking alone along a roadway at night, and in the distance you see a stranger approaching you. Whether you stop or change your direction or continue on will depend at first—in part—on your attitude, in this case how you feel about meeting up with strangers on dark roads at night.

Now, let us say that as you get closer you begin to see the stranger a little more clearly, and as you get even closer you find that you know who this person is—it is someone you recognize.

In this example, we can see that your *attitude*

about approaching the stranger was one thing, while your *perception* of the stranger was another thing entirely; in fact, your perception of the stranger changed the closer you got and the more clearly you could see him. Eventually, as you saw that you recognized the other person as a friend, you moved from having a perception of a potentially negative experience to dealing with a safer or potentially positive experience.

In the same way, that is how your perception of any change can strongly influence what you do about it. Is the change a foe or a friend? Like the stranger on the road, the closer you get, the clearer you can see—and the greater the perception of the change you will have.

■ Elevate the Change to a Better Level

You actually have a great deal to say about which category any change fits into. One of the first and most important steps you can take toward excelling in a time of change is to consciously determine for yourself how you want to *perceive* the change that's happening.

You can say that when the car breaks down and needs to be replaced, it is going to cost you more money, and that means this change—even though this could be a relatively minor change—is a Change of Limitation. And it's true, it could look like the extra strain on the budget represents only a problem, with no real benefit attached to it.

Or you could—*if you choose*—immediately start making a mental or written list of how this change is going to affect you in a *beneficial* way. You could choose to turn it into a Change of Progression. We know this works because it is practiced habitually—as a *way of life*—by people who are the most successful.

The man who says, "I really don't want to get this new car right now," and is upset that the old car has broken down, is really saying, "I don't want to accept this change, and I see it as a Change of Limitation." But then the man reworks his finances and finds a way to fit the new car into his monthly budget. Two weeks later he is driving a shiny new automobile, and he wouldn't part with it for anything. He has seen the truth: that getting the new car was a Change of Progression—because eventually, he made the choice to see it that way.

■ The First Step

Our objective in this section is to learn to begin taking changes out of the Changes of Limitation category, and start putting them under the heading of Changes of Progression. This is the process in which you begin to look for the *assets* in the change instead of dwelling on the *liabilities*.

There is a technique that will help you put this step into practice, and it is a technique that I have seldom seen fail. The next time you are confronted by any significant change that looks to be a Change of Limitation, ask three or four people who are successful, achievement-oriented individuals to suggest some ideas to you that will help you turn the change into an asset—a Change of Progression. I have never seen a potentially harmful change fail to give way to a defense of good positive ideas.

The reason this works is that when you are going

through the change, you may be busy dealing with the difficulties of it, and you may not have all the answers and all the solutions laid out in advance. People who are outside of the change but who have empathy and knowledge in their own specific areas can serve as expert short-term advisors. You may not need to rely on outside advice and opinions for the next change that comes along, but trying this technique even once or twice should convince you that there are always alternatives and there are always solutions.

With that frame of mind, there are few changes that are ultimately true Changes of Limitation. The first step is to start recognizing that with few exceptions, almost any change can be a Change of Progression. It is important to learn that the solutions are already there, even before you go looking for them.

21

Breaking Away from Average

Here is a short list of things that have occurred in the lives of "average" people. See if you can find what these changes had in common:

A mother came to live with her grown son and daughter-in-law. An administrative assistant at the office achieved a lifelong goal when she took a cassette course and learned to speak French. A man suffered a heart attack but proved to be healthy enough to be back at work with the same heavy schedule six weeks later. A young working couple moved across town to a larger apartment to make room for the arrival of their first child. A third-year college student changed his major from engineering to business. A woman finally decided to lose weight, and she joined a local weight-loss program and successfully lost thirty-seven pounds in three months. A man attended a seminar on personal organization and learned techniques that could add hours to his available time every week.

Each of those circumstances represents a fairly important change in someone's life. And even though all of those changes are somewhat different from each other, they do have something in common. In each of the cases, the change that took place represented a clear opportunity to take a major step forward in life.

But not all opportunities are fully taken advantage of. Take the examples above: The couple whose mother moved in with them had the opportunity to really get close to her for the first time ever. They didn't; in fact, they resented her being there.

The young woman who took the French lessons had first set her goal to learn French so that she could travel abroad and expand her horizons. She took the course, learned the language fairly well, and never left her hometown.

The man who had the heart attack had told himself just two days after it happened that some things were going to change—beginning with his impossible work schedule. A few weeks later he was right back at it. The couple who moved to the new apartment to make room for the birth of their child ended up with nothing more than an additional bedroom with bright pink and blue wallpaper. The young man who changed his college major from engineering to business thought it would probably change his life in the long run, but didn't notice much more than a change in professors after he re-enrolled.

The woman who lost thirty-seven pounds in three months had gained most of it back six months later. The man who decided to dedicate his life to getting more organized after he attended the seminar kept himself perfectly organized for exactly two weeks and two days. A year later he is still intending to get back at it.

The change comes, the people live through it, and life goes on—with only minor differences, *without any real change at all.*

A few chapters earlier we learned the story of Alexander, and how major changes had created a turning point in his life. He was met by a messenger of change called *personal growth,* and he experienced an awakening of enough intensity that it gave him the opportunity to change his future in a profound and positive way.

Few of us want to be struck by lightning—have our lives turned around so completely that we are finally ready to make a break for it, listen to the messenger of change, and do something exceptional with the rest of our lives.

The problem is that if we take our changes in stride, *without seeing them for what they really offer,* and fail to seize them as opportunities to create our own future, the changes come and go—and we never really get past average.

But what is it we do instead? We wait. We do okay. We do our best to deal with what happens. We mark off the days on the calendar—and the weeks and months and years go by. We may not spend a lot of time thinking about what it really means to *excel,* but then, on the other hand, we do well enough to get by. On the average—life is average.

So why try to break away from that? After all, what is wrong with average? We can tell ourselves that some people do a lot worse. So we reassure ourselves that we ought to feel pretty good just getting through life, even if we don't really make the most of it.

What is wrong with average is that it is *average.* It

is the easy way out. Accepting the average as the best way to live is like casting a vote for mediocrity, and even the vote is cast passively, without even thinking about it.

Deciding to "get out of average" is one of those choices that many will never make. They will think about it now and then, when they are inspired to achieve by something they read in a book or by something they learn in a motivational seminar, but their old past programs of indifference and inertia will stop all but a few of them from ever doing anything about it.

And yet, the step of moving from average to becoming an "individual" is not as difficult as it might seem. You can choose to live a life that protects the status quo and encourages complacency, or you can choose to make your life one that is full of vitality, promise, and enthusiasm for living. It takes no more time to do the one than to do the other. Why live one year of averageness and complacency when, in that same 365 days, you could live a year of personal rewards and fulfillment?

The choice, then, is this: *How would you really like to spend the next year of your life*—or the next five years, or the next ten? Many people genuinely *want* to move beyond where they are, they want to begin to excel—but they have no idea how to go about actually *living* that kind of life.

It is clear that the solution to the problem of "getting out of average" has to start with your decision to make the best possible choices in life—particularly the small, seemingly unimportant choices that affect the details of what you do hour by hour, day in and day out.

The next step—and one that is just as important—is the decision to take advantage of the natural changes that take place in your life in a far greater, more self-controlled way than you might ever have done before.

These "natural" changes are those inevitable changes that happen to each of us in the course of a normal life—changes like loss, separation, and change in location. You can make the choice to control the unavoidable changes that *will* happen to you, instead of allowing the changes to set your direction for you.

The process of moving from average to being an independent-thinking individual takes place when you begin to change the way you see yourself. Are you standing on the sidelines as a passive spectator when change occurs? Or do you jump in, *take charge of the change*, and use it to your advantage?

▪ Putting Yourself in the Director's Chair

If tomorrow morning you receive a phone call from a movie producer, who tells you that he wants to make a major motion picture of the story of your life, what would you think? Would you think that it was a great idea, and that it would be a fascinating and interesting story filled with great scenes of overcoming the odds and rising to ultimate achievement? Or would you think the producer was crazy?

If the contract were negotiated and signed, and you had the right to change anything in the movie script of your life that you wanted to, what would you change? Or would you be willing to see your life put on film exactly the way you are living it, with no exaggeration or enhancement to make the movie look more interesting?

The question here is not whether your friends and the rest of the world would enjoy the story of your life as you have really lived it; the question is whether or not *you* would be completely satisfied with the movie that you saw.

In real life, it is the average person, the one who consciously or unconsciously accepts mediocrity as the norm, who sees himself as the spectator on the sidelines while the movie of his own life is being scripted and filmed. It is the *self*-motivated, *self*-directed individual who, upon realizing that he may be standing on the sidelines, has a breakthrough of awareness. He climbs over the barricade on the movie set, takes the script and the director's bullhorn in hand, and starts *taking control* of the making of his life story for *himself*.

It is important to recognize that no one ever truly excels in a time of change—either when they are dealing with changes in the world around them, or when they are dealing with changes in their own lives—*without deciding to sit in their own director's chair.*

When it comes to excelling in a time of change, people who take active control, and maximize the positive value that every new change represents to them, end up succeeding—while the bystanders who are content to fit in with the crowd get passed by.

When you see yourself in your looking glass and examine who you are and what you want and how you deal with the changes in your life, do you see a bystander, or do you see a director? When you look at yourself in a mirror, do you see someone who lets changes come and go and is content to stand by—while someone else writes the script and directs the show—or do you see someone who gets the most out of the opportunities of change?

If you want to excel in a time of change, make the choice to get out of *average*, think for yourself, and put your *own* goals into *action*.

22

Arming Yourself with Stronger Self-Esteem

When you look at yourself in the mirror, do you like the person you see? Could you say that the person you're looking at is your favorite person in the whole world? And how much do you care about that person?

The answers to those questions begin to identify what is perhaps the single most important part of making changes work in your life: your personal self-esteem. And it is self-esteem that is at the root of more failings—and more successes—than any other single human characteristic.

■ The Role of Self-Esteem in Dealing with Change

It is a fact of human behavior that low self-esteem creates events that work *against* you; high self-esteem creates events that work *for* you. That sounds simple, but it is the most consequential factor to consider in the entire subject of dealing with change. Overall, year after year, the single most influential factor in whether things work for you or not is your own personal self-esteem.

When things aren't going right for too long a time, look at your self-esteem, and you will find the beginning of your answer. When things work well for you and continue to go well, look to your self-esteem to find out why.

Why is the development of stronger self-esteem so important to learning to excel in a time of change? The answer is simple and worth remembering: *You will succeed in life only to the extent that you care about youself.* You will excel in anything you do only to the extent that you believe you *deserve* to succeed. If it doesn't exist "in here," it cannot exist "out there."

Because of this, it is possible (and typical) for someone to want the best, set good goals, and try very hard to reach them, only to discover that attaining any lasting success becomes nothing more than an illusion. That is why it is so easy for some people to become so inspired by a book or a talk or some personal encouragement and then lose all the inspiration and the dreams a day or two later as completely as if they had never existed.

It is because your vision of yourself on the inside must be as big as the dreams you want to achieve. Your self-identity must be sculpted and shaped and nurtured and loved, day after day, year after year—and then the picture of yourself that you carry in your mind will be real enough and strong enough to create the successes that you deserved in the first place.

■ Your Self-Esteem Controls Your Results

It may not seem that something as basic as your self-esteem is going to control the results of everything you do—but it does. Your self-esteem is the picture of you that you carry around with you in your mind—it is the *you* who you believe yourself to be. Your self-esteem is supreme in its power; it is the most powerful ally or enemy that you've got. If your self-esteem is injured or low, *it will bring you down to its level*. If your self-esteem is strong, healthy, and high, *it will bring you up to its level*. So what you think about yourself dictates your success in everything you do.

If you think you deserve something, and your self-esteem is up to it, it will unconsciously help you take every appropriate action to get it. But if the picture of yourself that you carry in your mind is a limited picture, and you cannot see yourself as being able to achieve what you want, that program in your brain will do everything in its power to see that you do not reach your goal.

This is why there is so much attention today being given to the teaching of self-esteem to children. We want our children to grow up, be healthy, set goals, achieve success, and live happy lives—but we have learned that they can do none of those things well if their own self-esteem is not strong enough.

Fortunately, even if we were not raised with strong self-esteem, we can develop it as adults; it's not too late. We can learn to regain lost self-esteem, or we can even learn how to create it.

Self-esteem, like so many of the mental regulators that direct our behavior, is the result of our programming. As we have discussed, programming plays the central role in our overall success as individuals—both on a lifelong basis and day to day. But if you were to work on improving only one facet of your programming, the place to start would be your self-esteem. No matter how much of the right kind of self-esteem you have now, you can always use more of it. And no matter how it has been injured, or how much of it might have been lost in the past, it is never too late to build it back.

I have spent several years writing and speaking about the exciting discoveries in the field of neuroscience, and how we are using our new knowledge of the human brain to be able to replace harmful programs with healthy ones. During that time I have stood in front of audiences and watched many different people come to one surprising conclusion: They discovered that what they thought was the "problem" in their lives—was not the real problem at all! The real problem in almost every case was an inaccurate picture of themselves printed in their subconscious mind—a picture that caused them to see themselves as ultimately lacking and potentially failing. In short, the real problem was self-esteem.

▪ *The Genesis of Self-Esteem*

An in-depth study of human behavior and personal motivation reveals that much of what we do and how well things work out for us is the result of a sequence of events. When we understand this sequence of events, we gain insight into the basic mechanism that creates our success or failure in dealing with change. I will summarize the sequence for you:

1. We are "programmed" from birth.

From the day we are born, each of us receives programs—that become physiological "imprints" in the brain—from our parents, brothers and sisters, teachers, friends, all of our experiences, and from our own conscious and unconscious Self-Talk.

2. The programs we receive create our beliefs.

Along with the imprinted mental programs that tell us what we believe about the rest of the world and everything around us, we are given programs that we come to accept as the "true" picture of who we are, what we're made of, and how much value and worth we have. The messages others give us, and what we tell ourselves *about ourselves* is what our subconscious mind accepts as the truth about us—whether what we are programmed to believe is true or not.

3. Our programs determine our self-esteem.

Strong positive programs create strong positive self-esteem. Negative programs create low self-worth and low self-esteem.

**4. We always unconsciously attempt to live *up* to

or live *down* to the level of self-esteem that we are programmed to have.

This is the principal mechanism that determines our attitudes, our direction, our goals, and our ability to reach them. We can only reach—*and hold on to*—as high a level of success as our programs tell us we can. *To have success and to keep it, our self-esteem has to see us as worthy and deserving of that success in the first place.*

5. The way we react to any change is a direct result of our programmed level of self-esteem.

People who consistently react to change in a negative way, or who see change as filled with problems or as being unlucky or unfair, do so because of their own reduced level of self-esteem—and their own *perceived inability* to deal with change in a positive way and to deserve positive results. That is the result of low self-esteem.

People who see change as opportunity and trust their ability to deal with it and enhance their lives as a result of it are able to do so because of higher levels of personal self-esteem.

6. Self-esteem can be built and improved, even in adults.

A conscious program of personal self-improvement can create clear and positive results in the level of your own self-esteem. How you feel about yourself today, as an example, can be modified or improved by practicing mental self-esteem-building exercises.

7. The results of improving self-esteem show up in all of an individual's attitudes and actions.

The direct result of higher self-esteem is improved performance in all activities, more successful goal achievement, and improved overall accomplishment and self-approval.

We may not yet fully understand the magnitude of the role that our own individual self-esteem plays in our lives. Even after working for many years in the field of motivational behavior, which deals with the development of self-esteem, I am still amazed at what this one facet of our lives controls. There is certainly no doubt that an accurate summary of human behavior would include this single basic fact: Whatever we have stored in our own brain about ourselves—consciously and subconsciously—is what we believe to be true and what we will act out; we do everything based on the pictures of ourselves that our own chemically and electrically imprinted programs have stored in our minds.

That same idea—*that we become what we believe about ourselves*—has been stated and restated in many ways since the earliest philosophies of mankind were first recorded. Most recently, the study of the human brain—and how neurological programs in the brain determine our attitudes and actions—has proved this centuries-old belief to be true. Now we know that the *process* for this exists—and it is *physiological*. It is not just some philosophical idea or little-understood gem of wisdom; it is a chemical and electrical, neurological component of the human brain.

Your behavior and mine are based on that chemistry. And the self-esteem that we have—or do not have—that drives us to achieve or forces us to fail is the result of that same chemistry.

That's very good news! That means that if our own chemistry is working against us because the pictures in our computer control center are the wrong kinds of pictures, we can do something about it! We have learned that we *can* change the programs that set up and control our self-esteem. It takes practice to build stronger self-esteem, but we can do it—and it has been proved time and again that it works.

Fixing injured self-esteem can be simple or it can be a long process, depending on how strong the old programs are. But the basis of all *effective* self-esteem-improvement methods is *practice*. Learning about self-esteem, or understanding it intellectually, doesn't do the job. It helps you to become more aware of the processes involved in how self-esteem works, but understanding it and having it are two entirely different things.

■ The Source of Self-Esteem

There are people who have a *high* degree of understanding when it comes to knowing how self-esteem works, but still have a *low* degree of self-esteem. It helps to understand how self-esteem works, but if you want more of it, or if you want to improve your own self-esteem, the solution can come only from practice.

Good self-esteem comes primarily from one of these three sources:

a. Hearing good things about yourself
b. Thinking good things about yourself
c. Doing something that you are proud of

There are those who might say that there are many sources of self-esteem—but most of those sources eventually boil down to one of those three conditions taking place. You are receiving positive approval and positive pictures of yourself from someone else, or you are doing something or accomplishing something that causes you to acknowledge something good about yourself.

■ Your Self-Esteem Changes How You Deal with Change

In order to be able to consistently recognize the potential good in change, and to consistently see it through and make it happen, it is paramount that you give yourself the strongest, healthiest self-esteem that you possibly can. There is nothing that can take the place of having strong self-esteem—and there is nothing that works better than *consciously* building it.

Over the years, I have been asked to outline the best steps for building self-esteem that I have found. There are a lot of ideas that have been tried, but there are only a few that have proved to work time after time.

For the purposes of this book, I have compiled the best of these and outlined them in simplified form. Since self-esteem is the single most important component in successfully dealing with change, I would recommend that you actively practice building your self-esteem (no matter how much of it you have already) while you are practicing turning new changes into personal successes.

■

■ PERSONAL EXERCISES ■
A Basic Self-Esteem Workout

---

1. Use "Self-Talk" that always builds more Self-Esteem.

Every thought you say to yourself—either consciously or unconsciously—is adding new programs to your brain. Because of past programming, as much as three-fourths of what we actually say to ourselves (even without thinking about it) is negative and destroys self-esteem! Remember, the programs you give yourself are being chemically and electrically imprinted in your brain, and each of those programs contributes to your overall picture of yourself. You're in charge of your programming; make sure your own Self-Talk always builds you up and never puts you down.

2. Each morning, when you look in the mirror, tell yourself out loud that you choose to spend that day building your self-esteem.

Start the day by making yourself aware that your own self-esteem is important to you. The self-esteem you build is going to affect everything else that you do, day after day.

3. Carry an index card in your pocket that says the words "I build self-esteem in everything I do." Take the card out and read it now and then during the day.

This appears to be an awfully simple thing to do, but that is undoubtedly why it works so well. It's simple; it doesn't take any extra time or effort, and yet doing this one thing can be so effective that you can actually see and feel the results during the day.

4. Never allow yourself the negative luxury of doing anything that could possibly diminish your self-esteem in any way.

Some of the things that hurt self-esteem are negative Self-Talk, unhealthy or harmful habits, arguing, hurting someone else—emotionally or otherwise—complaining, and failing to take positive action when you know you should. Doing the opposite of these is what builds self-esteem.

Always talk to yourself in the most believing and caring way. Even if it feels strange at first to tell yourself wonderfully positive things about yourself, understand that the strange feeling is just your old disbelieving programs trying to argue against you. Be good to yourself, treat yourself with respect, and always treat other people with respect. Use your integrity; tell the truth, and also be honest with yourself.

Build other people up, and show them the best of themselves. When you do that, you help remind yourself of the qualities that you have. When you are supportive and understanding instead of arguing or demeaning, you give yourself some very strong programs—of the right kind.

Everything you do in any given day is actually practicing behaviors that make your life either work—or not work. If you want to have more self-esteem, practice doing the things that give it to you. Practice not doing the things that take it away.

5. Learn the right kind of Self-Talk. If you can, listen to Self-Talk cassettes that build self-esteem, and when you can't listen, repeat the same kind of Self-Talk to yourself.

That, too, sounds like a simple thing to do, but try it and watch what happens. Don't just try it for a day or two and expect to see a miraculous change in your life. If you aren't listening to the phrases on a cassette, then repeat the phrases silently throughout the day—each time you meet someone else, or when the telephone rings, or when you see yourself in the mirror—anytime you remind yourself to do so—repeat the phrases consistently, in a way that you will remember to say the words to yourself. Keep doing that for a minimum of three to four weeks to get started developing the habit.

Can listening to cassette tapes of Self-Talk phrases or repeating phrases like "I like myself; I have self-esteem!" actually create more self-esteem? Yes, it can. We are fortunate; that is how the brain works.

If you want to do more work in this area, I recommend that you spend extra time on this. Make it a project, and set a goal, and spend the next 90 days (or the next 12 months) getting good at building self-esteem. But above all, don't skip a day—and make building self-esteem a habit. There is only one way to actually build self-esteem for yourself—and that is to practice building it.

23

Metamorphosis— Getting Ready to Make It Work

We have all seen the negative effects of what happens when we don't deal with change well; now let's look at what can happen when we learn to do it right.

In the past few years we have learned in the field of personal motivation that one of the most important elements in making positive changes in our own lives is having a good role model to follow. The more clearly we can see success actually happening, and the more we can identify with that success happening in our own lives, the more we pattern our own behavior after it. It is from learning more about the mental programming process of the brain that we have learned the value of creating clear pictures of a positive self-identity.

We have learned that the more you see yourself living and acting and thinking in a certain way, the more you will tend to live out that picture of yourself. So the old adage that "you end up becoming what you think you" are is put into actual practice when you *choose* how to see yourself and then make it *happen*.

If, in the story we read earlier, Alexander had had an entirely different picture of himself that he could look at, and think about, and practice seeing all that time, it is certain that he would *not* have ended up believing that his life was worthless and that he had nothing to live for.

What actually happened when the messenger of change came was that Alexander was given a *new picture* of himself to look at, and even as he saw the picture for the first time, we saw the beginning moments of a transformation in his life.

■ Giving Yourself the Right Picture of You

It is unlikely that a stranger is going to walk up to you and show you a completely wonderful picture of yourself and your marvelous future. So I'm going to give you that wonderful picture—to carry around with you and to begin to live out.

To create the right kind of picture of yourself in your mind, it is important to see yourself having *already* accomplished your goal. In this case, we're going to see you dealing with every single change in your life in the most positive and successful way. What you are doing by reading—and *re*reading—the following description, is giving yourself a *completed picture of you* so that you have a clear role model of your most successful self to follow.

As you read this description, make the decision to

suspend disbelief and put your doubts away for a while. Let yourself see the best picture of you that there could possibly be. That's a healthy thing to do. It lets you see yourself at your best, and it reminds you of that incredible potential within you that is waiting to live in the rest of your life. So when you read the description, see it as actually being *you*. "Listen" to it as though you are hearing someone describe you as you actually are. This is a description that *is* accurate and true—this is a picture that is all about you.

Living Through Change with Incredible You

You really are incredible! You deal with change exceptionally well! You make change a positive, practical force in your life. You feel good about yourself. You like who you are, and you deal with change well because you have strong, healthy self-esteem.

You are a person of worth and value. And every day you work to create even greater quality and value in your life. So you build your self-esteem, and you keep it strong. Each morning you look at yourself in the mirror and you give yourself the powerful words of Self-Talk that say

"I like myself. I have self-esteem."
"I like myself. I have self-esteem."
"I like myself. I have self-esteem."

And self-esteem is just one of the many qualities that you possess that help you excel in the changes in your life.

You also take *personal responsibility* for yourself. That means you take control of who you are, what you do, what you say, how you think, and where you're going. You never let changes control you or lead you away from your goals.

You think well. You have a good mind. You organize your thoughts. You and you alone are responsible for what you think and how you think, so you always make sure that you give yourself the very best messages for your own mind. You never allow yourself to think thoughts that could harm you, hold you back, or work against you in any way.

When you have to make a change, and you want to make that change work for you, your own positive, winning attitude lets you know that you *can* do it. When a change of any kind happens to you—even a change that you may not have wanted—you face it, you deal with it, you learn from it—and with your attitude, you overcome it!

You are *good* at handling changes. Right now see yourself dealing with a change and achieving more because of it. See yourself creating opportunities or tackling the problem, and see yourself winning. No matter what it is, you *can* deal with it—you can *excel* because of it, and you know you can.

When it comes to dealing with a problem of any kind, you take action. You never put things off, and you do everything you need to do when you need to do it. Because you set goals, you know where you are headed, so you know what to do next. Instead of waiting around and wondering what to do, you find the answers you need—and you put yourself into motion.

When you need help, you get it—but you never rely on someone else to motivate you or to take your action for you. And you know that with your personal strength and courage, you can get through anything. You have what it takes, and you know you do. And you make sure you let yourself know it.

Because you make things happen, you create the right kind of changes in your life, and you make them work for you. And when changes happen, with or without your design, you make them happen *for* you. In the long run, you make sure that every change happens for the best.

You turn changes of loss into new chances to learn from life and to appreciate what you have. You turn changes of separation into a time of thankfulness for what is yours to keep and hold. You turn relocation into renewal and the chance to experience more of life. You see changes in relationships as a natural part of living and growing, and you always work to make your relationships rich and rewarding.

You always see a change in direction as a time to expand your horizons, and to use even more of your talents and skills. You make sure that you create the kinds of changes in your life that give you better health, and you see any change in your health as a reminder to do everything you can to keep yourself fit and full of vitality. And you see every positive change in your own personal growth as an exceptional gift that you have given yourself.

An accurate description of you would include the words *intelligent, strong, self-directed, confident, calm, capable, competent, level-headed, willing to learn, interested, energetic, full of enthusiasm, optimistic, happy, full of spirit, determined, alert, full of life,* and *ready to take action.*

You *are* good at dealing with change! You have made the choice to excel in your own time of change, each day and in every way. You are *incredible,* and today's a great day to show it!

* * *

Just imagine seeing *that* picture of yourself every day! Imagine having that kind of self-belief and, as a result, that kind of self-direction. That attitude makes one want to say, "Go ahead, changes—*I'm ready for you!* I'm ready for anything—*I can handle it!*"

If you would like to know what goes on in the mind of a person who is happy, successful, achieving, and emotionally very healthy, reread the words that are written in this section, and you will know the kinds of thoughts and self-belief that live within that person's mind.

It may help you to mark the previous pages in this book and come back to them from time to time and read them again. Try reading them through just before you go to sleep at night and watch what happens. The more you become familiar with those words, the more you will begin to notice that they really *are* written about you. If you read them often, even once or twice a week, you will begin to notice that you and your thinking are becoming more like the description.

■ What Do You See in the Looking Glass?

What you see when you look into the looking glass at yourself—what you see in your own mind once you are aware of your ability to create your own image of yourself—will always be the result of what you choose to put there. Since what you choose to nourish yourself with will always be up to you, there is no good reason not to nourish yourself with the best. If you do that one thing—take care of *the picture of you* first and always—then you can be sure that you will always be able to deal with change and make the *best* of it.

Think of someone whom you would describe as successful in every important way, and who is what we would call *together*, and who is clearly happy and fulfilled. This is the kind of person that you could look at and say, "That is how I would like to be; that is how I would like to feel about my life."

Then imagine someone else saying those same things about you, and looking up to you for the way you have chosen to live *your* life, and for the kind of person you are. The final step of metamorphosis, the final step of truly coming to life, is a step that awaits the *choice* of those who want to do it. It is a wonderful choice to make—and you already have what it takes to make that choice for yourself.

PART FIVE

How to Excel in a Time of Change

24

Putting the Process into Practice

Now it's time to do something with what we've learned. It's time to take action.

We have taken a close look at change. We have seen the role that it played in ancient history. We have seen change in later times as it began to form and shape our culture, and we have watched change build to such a frenzied pace that it is all we can do to keep up with it.

And we are aware that there is more change to come—a lot more—and that we are just now seeing only the beginning of the real changes that lie ahead. Understanding a broader picture of where we came from, and how we arrived at this precise moment in history—in the midst of a greater time of change than we have ever known—gives us a clearer perspective from which to understand where we fit in the scheme of things. It helps us recognize what changes to anticipate in our own lives because of the massive changes around us.

When we looked at our own future, we saw more change coming than perhaps we would like to admit. But it is also clear that along with the change, there is a lot of good in store for all of us. So we are encouraged not only to be ready for the changes that are still to come, but to take advantage of a time that suggests unparalleled opportunity for personal and professional growth.

We have been introduced to the seven Major Changes—"messengers" who, when they come calling, bring with them the most important changes that we experience in our lives. We learned that these messengers can be identified and recognized, and perhaps even made friends with. Learning to identify those changes can give us a lot of help in dealing with them. They are inevitable; they visit all of us, and knowing the identity of each of them expands our knowledge of change and brings with it the benefit of preparedness.

So we looked at each Major Change, and got to know it—and the next time one of them arrives, we'll know what we're dealing with. An understanding of the seven Major Changes alone can make the whole process of dealing with change a lot easier. It is one of those times when the more you know, the more you win.

After identifying the major changes in our lives, and learning to recognize them, we learned a process that would help us deal with change in a better way. The six steps of Recognition, Acceptance or Rejection, Choosing Your Attitude, Choosing Your Style, Choosing Your Action, and Review and Evaluation make it possible for you to take more control in dealing with most of the changes in your life. And we then took a look into a very personal mirror to see how we view change personally, and how it has been affecting us.

■ | *Turning Knowledge into Action*

In time, as I have studied the ideas that offer us more successful ways to live, I have come across many good ideas. But, I have also found that all too many of the ideas fall short—they stop before they actually get anything done. What starts out as a truly helpful concept too often ends up just as words that may get printed in a book but go no further.

It wasn't that the concepts did not have merit; many of the concepts have been good! But in each case, the difference between the great ideas that actually worked for people and those ideas that did not, was that only a few of them contained within them the means to put the concept into actual *practice*. It is again a case of knowledge by itself being worth little. Unless you can do something with what you have learned, all you have really done is to have learned *about* something. You've learned it, but you haven't *experienced* it.

Without exception, every successful self-help concept I have ever encountered had within it the means by which to put it into *immediate* practice. But even once practiced, some good ideas still fall into disuse—and like the once-read books now sitting on the shelf, the good idea that could have worked became nothing more than a moment or two of uneventful motivation. It is like a spark that should have ignited into a bright, burning flame, but instead, for the lack of a hand to fan the flame, it slowly died out.

So, too, making the choice to learn *about* change becomes no more than a brief flicker of insight if you do not add a *second* choice. And that second choice is to turn discovery into action. That means that if you put together your thoughts and ideas about change and, in the process, make a discovery or two, you will likely only *retain* those discoveries *if you practice them for yourself.*

In dealing with the changes in your life, you can do one of two things: You can *learn* about change but never make any personal commitment to do anything about it yourself. Or you can practice looking at the changes differently and then make the choice to *deal* with those changes by using a logical plan of action.

▪ *Make the Decision to Try It for Yourself*

In the next two chapters I have suggested two tools for you to use. They are tools that I have seen put into action time after time, and each time they have been practiced, I have watched them work.

If you would like to see the same ideas work for you, getting started will take little more than your choice to do so. How well they work for you will depend entirely on the depth of that choice. The more determined you are, the more results you will see.

Remember that your own past programming may try to work against you. Any negative program you hold will do everything it possibly can to prove to you that whatever it is you are trying will not work, or that it is for someone else but not for you, or that you don't need to practice new ideas because you already have all of your skills mastered.

By seducing us into believing that we can put off the future and never really have to face it—or, worse yet, by convincing us that we are not cut out to be much better than we already are—our old programs try to put us to sleep and tell us, *"It's okay. Why work at it! Why bother!"*

And then our old programs add those classic words that have stopped so many from achieving, when they say: *"It probably won't work anyway!"* Or your old programming will point out to you that you've tried something similar before and you failed or it did not work. Or it will suggest that you don't have the time right now, and that this is something else you can easily put off for later. And your old programming will get you to put off using the tools for a tomorrow that it tries to tell you will never come.

■ *Getting Past the Old Programs*

In nearly every personal workshop that I have conducted, one of the questions that I have been asked most often is how can we overcome negative programs that work against us. It's a good question to ask. The old programs can be so subtle, so quiet, that we're sometimes not even aware of what is being whispered to us. We don't recognize how insidious and self-destructive the messages quietly dredged up from the dark past programs of our subconscious minds can be. And those programs probably weren't even of our own doing. But we got them, one by one—almost without notice—from people around us who didn't quite understand the importance of the "care and feeding" of our subconscious minds.

If you want to defeat something within you that is trying to hold you back, the answer always lies in the word *practice*. So I encourage you to use the tools, and to practice. Practice may not make perfect, but if we practice taking the right steps, we certainly get a lot closer to getting better. The more you replace habits and attitudes that have worked against you in the past, with habits and attitudes that work *for* you, the greater the chance you have of winning the most important competition you will ever engage in.

The next step is to make sure that the key *directions*—the most significant messages—that we give to ourselves, are the right directions.

The most effective method for setting, maintaining, and *controlling* our direction in life is through the use of specific *self*-directions. And that begins with the use of the right *words*. In the next chapter we'll take a look at some of the most important words that we can ever use. Learning to use them not only gives us powerful messages about who we are and where we are going—it also gives us a powerful tool that we can use to make sure we get there.

25

The Ten Most Important
Words of Change

Words can be powerful symbols. Words are legions of metaphors that march through our minds. They command us, conquer us, and subdue us—or they defend us, give us our strength, and lead us to our victories. Mightier than both the sword and the pen is the *word* itself.

For many years, as I studied and observed the amazing ability of one mind to think its way to success while another mind, similar in every apparent way, thought itself into failure, I began to recognize the profound importance that certain individual words were playing in those successes or failures. I watched hundreds of people consciously choose a road that was leading them to happiness and success—and I watched hundreds of other individuals struggle and flail—and succeed only at failure.

I listened to both kinds of people very carefully. I listened to every word and every nuance of every word that they spoke. As I listened, I began to sense that it was not the victory or the defeat that was creating the words those people were saying to themselves; *it was the other way around:* The words they were using were literally *creating* their successes or failures for them!

So I began to study the vocabularies of the winners and the vocabularies of the nonwinners and the vocabularies of all those in between. I studied the words and the thoughts of everyone I met. Over a long period of time my observations presented undeniable evidence that certain of the words that each of the individuals were using were directly tied not only to the rest of their thoughts, but to their attitudes, their actions, and the results of those actions. In short, their successes or failures were clearly directed by no more than a basic "vocabulary of self-identity"—*a few basic words* that each of them used frequently.

▪ *The Discovery*

To me, that was a breakthrough of incredible proportions. On one hand, it appeared as though I had discovered something that was so simple, it couldn't be of any significance at all. On the other hand, with my continuing interest in the discoveries that were being made in the anatomy of the human mind, I could see that there was a clear tie between the *vocabulary* that each person used and the successes or the failures that those words were creating. And it was a connection that was ultimately *physiological.* That is, there was a direct interaction between certain words of common vocabulary and a physiological—an electrical and chemical—response to those words in the brain.

In time I began to see these common words as unique, or set apart from other words, in that they gave exceptionally strong instructions to the brain; in a sense, they were like trigger words. The full depth and intent of their meaning lay so far buried in the subconscious mind of the individuals who used them that people did not understand the impact that the repeated use of those few words were having on their thoughts, on their attitudes, and on their behavior.

I observed that people who were clearly in the category of "those who are successful" used one group of words frequently, habitually, every day. And they were words that the "less than successful" or the "failure" group *almost never used!*

The reverse was also true. Those people who were having a lot of difficulties consistently used words that were clearly self-effacing or even self-destructive. The "failure" group regularly used words that were almost never used by the people in the "success" group.

A common trap to a behavioral researcher would be to automatically assume that the person who is successful would naturally feel better about himself, and as a result, he would naturally use more positive-sounding words. In a similar way, it could appear that the person who is struggling and failing would fall into a state of self-defeat that would cause him to think in darker tones, and that the words he used to express himself would be a reflection of that failure and the anxiety that went along with it.

■ The Answer

It was in the "middle" group of people, those who were neither doing especially well or especially poorly, that I looked for the answer. What I found was that in almost every case that I observed, *the vocabulary preceded the result*. The words people used when they expressed themselves *preceded* the results they experienced.

Those in the average group who began to practice using more positive words in their vocabularies began to *act out* the descriptions and the actions that those new words implied!

Those who began to talk down to themselves began, in time, to follow their own words with less successful actions. Those who learned to talk themselves up, in time began to find that their successes were increasing almost in direct proportion to the frequency with which they used the new "success-oriented" words.

Upon reflection, it seems that the importance of "symbol words" should have been clear to everyone all along. If this had been the case, I suspect that long ago we would have used the knowledge to deal more effectively with the prevention of a lot of personal problems that we bring upon ourselves—and have to deal with in every area of our lives.

But at least we are now finally beginning to understand how the process works: Words are symbols to the brain. Those symbols—when presented to the brain—open up huge file drawers of beliefs and conceptions that are previously—and permanently—stored in the brain. Some words open up file drawers that are filled with pictures of achievement and personal accomplishment. Other words are symbols that open up file drawers that are filled with beliefs of self-doubt and inadequacy.

We are finally beginning to understand the value of those certain specific words—and the mental images that the use of those words create in the mind. They have almost unimaginable influence in our lives—so much influence that it is quite possible that these words may play the single, final deciding role in an individual's personal fight for accomplishment and fulfillment.

■ | *It's in the Words*

Throughout the time that I studied the use of single, forceful words as strong mental "programmers," I had a goal to compile a complete list of the most essential of these words, and to write and define them in a book. I recently reached that goal when I completed a book entitled *100 Golden Words*. In that book I included the first 100 of the words that I now believe to be so important that I consider them among the most important "gifts" that any of us could ever give to ourselves.

I have selected a few of those words—ten of them that apply directly to dealing with change and controlling your life—to share with you here. They are very simple words, and yet they are filled with strong, healthy images full of life-giving energy—and so full of the pictures of self-accomplishment and fulfillment! They are some of the best "symbols" or directions that we could ever give to the control centers of our minds.

These are words that, if used often, practiced daily, and made to become a prominent part of our own everyday vocabularies, could not only make the changes we face go better for us; they could affect in an exceptionally positive and practical way everything else about us. When used and practiced and put to work with vision and enthusiasm, these words become the words of individual achievement and fulfillment.

I would like to share a few of those words with you now. Here are a few words that, when made a part of your everyday life, can help you excel in every area of your life, and most certainly in a time of change.

A FEW OF THE WORDS OF GREATNESS

1. ANTICIPATE

Anticipate means to expect and to get ready for. When it comes to getting ready for good things that are about to happen, there is no better word to use than *anticipate*. There is no other word in the English language that has more hope and promise and expectation built into it. If you use this word in the right way, and always remind yourself that to anticipate means to look forward to something good that is coming, you do yourself a great favor. You get ready to expect the best.

To anticipate is to be alive! Among all of the words that describe the events that happen in our lives, the word *anticipate* stands alone in its description of an almost unlimited expectation. To the achiever, to anticipate is to look forward to life with hope and trust and belief.

The more you learn to anticipate any change and its results, the more in control you will be of what happens next. The opposite of the word *anticipate* is the word *ignore*—the root of the word *ignorance*. To anticipate is to be aware—in advance—of something that is happening in your life.

People who practice anticipating are people who are in touch with their lives and are aware of what's going on around them. The more you practice using this word in the most positive possible way, and the more you practice anticipating the likely events that will happen next, the more in control of your life you will be.

Some of the words that live closest to the word *anticipate* are: *foresight, intuition, awareness, preparedness,* and *confidence.*

In a Phrase:
"I anticipate, plan, and prepare. I am successful, and I am always ready, in the most positive possible way, for what lies ahead. I anticipate."

2. CHOICE
This word, used by those who have chosen to be successful, is one of the most respected words in the language of success. It is perceived to be a "right" by some, and something akin to a "responsibility" by others; but of all the words you will ever find to help you create a life of fulfillment and success, there is no greater word than the simple word *choice.*

To one who chooses to succeed and excel, the real meaning of *choice* is to take personal control over what you do with your self and your life. Making a personal choice is the single most *independent* thing you can ever do.

The word *choice* is the difference between a life that is lived by one's own direction and a life that is left up to chance. Of all the gifts that we are given in our lives, there is perhaps no greater gift than the power of independent personal choice.

It is as simple as the right to say "yes" to something that is good, or to say "no" to something that is wrong or harmful in our lives. And it is as complex as the right to determine and direct our destinies or—without choice—to leave that same destiny in the hands of chance or in the control of someone else.

The measure of your successes will always be the direct result of the *choices* that you make for yourself.

Some of the words that live closest to the word *choice* are: *alternatives, goal, objective, individual right, personal responsibility* and *self-determination.*

In a Phrase:
"I make choices. I choose my course of action in everything that I do. I create achievement and fulfillment in my life. I make choices!"

3. Belief/Believe
Of all the words that we might search for to inspire us to move forward in our lives, there is no greater word than *belief,* and no greater choice than to *believe.*

The greater assurances of *hope, faith,* and *promise* come to life within us because of our choice to *believe.* Those who succeed, and those who achieve their best, believe in their successes and their achievements—sometimes long before they see them. But the reason they achieve begins with the belief that they would.

Belief is among the most important driving forces that set the successful individual apart from those who fail. In the personal stories of our own lives, it is never the circumstances of our lives that ultimately determine our success or failure; it is our own belief in ourselves.

Some of the words that live closest to the words *belief* and *believe* are: *self-identity, self-esteem, choice, faith,* and *confidence.*

In a Phrase:
"I believe in myself. With my strength, my confidence, and my belief, I make achievement a way of life!"

4. CREATIVE/CREATIVITY

It is creativity that is at the heart of all newfound solutions. Even problems that would have seemed to be insurmountable give way when confronted with the strength of personal creativity.

Creativity is a gift that all of us are born with. Some people expand and enhance their creativity throughout their entire lives. Other people never understand what it is, or they believe that creativity is reserved for others. In failing to practice using their creativity, they lose it.

Creativity is engaged in by thinking about something in a new way. It is thinking a thought that you have not practiced thinking before. The starting point of all creativity is thought. All you have to do is consciously desire to create.

Creativity is something that does not happen by itself; it is generated when the mind is consciously focused on result while being left open far enough for inspiration to enter. Creativity is a state of mind that chooses to seek alternatives instead of shutting them out.

Some of the words that live closest to the words *creative* and *creativity* are: *imagination, inspiration, concentration, resourcefulness,* and *solution.*

In a phrase:
"I am creative. I always approach changes, problems, and opportunities in a creative and resourceful way. I have a good mind, and I use it well; I am very creative."

5. PERSPECTIVE

Perspective is the position from which you view life. Those people who are most in control of their own lives are aware of their perspective—a perspective they have chosen for themselves.

Perspective is created by a combination of beliefs and attitudes. People change their perspective by adding to their awareness and by adjusting their attitudes. A healthy perspective is always a broad perspective; the broader your perspective, the healthier and more helpful it will be to you.

Having a broad awareness of what's going on

in your life—keeping sight of the bigger picture—lowers your center of gravity and gives you firmer ground to stand on. In dealing with change, the broader your perspective, the greater the gale you can withstand without being swept away by the winds of change.

The healthiest of perspectives never stands in the same company with closed-mindedness, prejudice, conceit, shortsightedness, ignorance, opinion, or sanctimony.

A broad, healthy perspective is nurtured and strengthened by open-mindedness, curiosity, willingness to learn, and a relentless search for truth.

Some of the words that live closest to the word *perspective* are: *balance, insight, attitude, integrity,* and *awareness.*

In a phrase:
"I have perspective. I choose to see the world and everything around me in the clearest and broadest possible way. One of the reasons that I am strong and stable is because I choose to keep a healthy balance and a clear perspective in everything I think and do. I have perspective."

6. GOAL
This simple word of only four letters can do more to bring success and achievement into your life than even *knowledge, money,* and *fortune* combined. Those things help, but they create little lasting success without a goal to guide them.

It is the goal that shapes the plan; it is the plan that sets the action; it is the action that achieves the result; and it is the result that brings the success. And it all begins with the simple word *goal.*

Goals define our dreams and give structure to our futures. They harness our energies, focus our thoughts, and give us direction and purpose. A goal is more than a want, a wish, a desire, or a dream. A true goal is thought out, planned out, written out, and carried out.

Of all of the attributes that are found among people who create and hold on to success in their lives, the one single attribute that all of them have in common is that they set goals, write them down, review them regularly, and refuse to stop until they have reached them.

Some of the words that live closest to the word *goal* are: *determination, plan, timetable, action, review, direction, achievement,* and *success.*

In a phrase:
"I set goals. I think them through, I write them down, I review them each day, and I work to make them happen. I choose to be successful. I'm good at setting goals!"

7. Action

What a wonderful word—*action!* For those who choose to succeed, it means to put yourself into motion, to come to life, to get involved with your own sucess, and to get busy getting the right things done.

Action is *choice* in motion. And when action—of any kind—is called for, whether you take action or do not take action, will ultimately be up to the choice you make.

Taking positive action is something to be

proud of. There is no better feeling than when you are taking action. You know that you are doing something; you know that you are contributing, and because you have a goal and a plan, you know that you are doing something worthwhile. It is *action* that turns any good plan into *accomplishment*.

Action is a word that those who choose to achieve keep in the forefront of their minds, and they use it often. Somewhere close to every triumph and every victory, you will find action. There is no true accomplishment without it.

Some of the words that live closest to the word *action* are: *life, motion, energy, drive, enthusiasm, initiate, control,* and *solution.*

In a phrase:
"I take action. I put myself in motion. I know what to do, and I get things done. When action is called for, I always take action."

8. Achieve/Achievement

Along with the choice to succeed, the personal choice to *achieve* is the genesis of personal accomplishment. True achievement is never the result of accident; it is always the result of *desire* and *action.*

To achieve is to strive, surpass, and conquer. To be an achiever is to be one who stands apart from the crowd. It is the achiever who sets his horizons the farthest distance away but who is also willing to go the greatest distance to reach them.

In the language of success, achievement is one

of the few words that has no other meaning than one that is positive. To achieve is to *live*.

Some of the words that live closest to the word *achievement* are: *winning, successful, competence, confidence, challenge, self-esteem, pride, accomplishment, perseverance, value, contribution, worth,* and *happiness.*

In a phrase:
"I am an achiever. Achievement to me is a way of life. I add to my life and to the lives of others because I choose to achieve in every important thing I do. I have value and great worth, and it shows; I am an achiever!"

9. Adapt/Adaptive

The essential word *adapt* focuses on two important abilities for dealing with change. One is to be able to adapt ourselves to situations that are beyond our control; the other is to adapt situations around us so that the situation works for us in a more effective way.

It is in your ability to adapt—either yourself or the situation—that you will find the solution to overcoming most of the problems you will ever encounter. And it is the ability to adapt that offers you the deftness with which to respond to any situation in a more productive and worthwhile way.

When you choose to be adaptive, you are saying that you choose to be flexible, responsive, able to transcend and reform. The one who fails to adapt becomes the swordsman who fences with the world with his feet in chains. Choosing to be adaptive gives you the freedom to move, to modify, and to change—and all at your choice. When dealing with change, the art of adapting is almost always preferable to the necessity of compromise.

Some of the words that live closest to the word *adapt* and *adaptive* are: *accommodate, shape, acclimate, adjust,* and *transform.*

In a phrase:
"I adapt to any situation well, but always by my own choosing. And I am very good at adapting any situation to create the best possible outcome. I know how to adapt—and I know how to win!"

10. Excel

Excel is a special word that stands above all ohers. To excel is to surpass, to outshine, to lead, and to exceed. It is a word of eminence, superiority, and greatness; it is a word that instills in the bearer a feeling of worth and value and quality of being.

One of our greatest honors is that we are given the opportunity to *choose* to excel. It is a gift of choice that adds immeasurably to our lives.

It is when you make the conscious choice to excel that you first begin to reach forward to touch your true potential. Along with the discovery of one's own self, and the acknowledgment of the true spirit of living at your best, there can be no greater fulfillment than that which comes from choosing to *excel.* It adds to life a quality of living that outshines and stands above any other earthly endeavor.

Some of the words that live closest to the

word *excel* are: *transcend, actualize, self-direc-tion, exceptional, uncommon, character,* and *commitment.*

In a phrase:
"*I choose to excel, in times of change and throughout my life. I am a person of quality, value, and worth; I choose to excel!*"

These are just a few of the words of individual achievement and fulfillment. They are the basic tools of success. The more you make those words an active part of your daily life, the more your life will reflect the exceptional qualities that those essential, powerful words impart. Use them. Practice them. And watch the results that the *words* create.

■

■ **PERSONAL EXERCISES** ■

1. *Write out the ten words from this chapter. (See how many you can remember without referring to the previous pages.)*

(1) _____

(2) _____

(3) _____

(4) _____

(5) _____

(6) _____

(7) _____

(8) _____

(9) _____

(10) _____

2. *Write each word on a 3×5 index card. On the back of the card, write the words "I practice _____ (fill in the word) every day." Carry one card with you each day until you have practiced using all ten words.*

3. *For the next several days, reread the section of this chapter containing the ten words just before you go to sleep each night or the first thing when you wake up in the morning.*

26

Your Personal Book
of Changes

This next step in our process will help you create a practical plan for your personal management of change. **Your Personal Book of Changes** is part *assessment*, part *goal plan*, and part *action plan*.

Use this tool as a guide to help you identify key points that you want to focus on and spend time working with.

The purpose of **Your Personal Book of Changes** is to give you a *structure* to follow. And it will help you practice making changes more manageable. The more you practice going through the specific steps that help you organize the management of change, the more you will be able to break the change down into its component parts and deal with each one of them individually.

Your Personal Book of Changes is also a review of some of the essential ideas we have discussed and a reference guide for outlining the changes you want to work on at any time.

People who deal with change successfully recognize that one of the keys to dealing with change is the single habit of *practice*. Most of us can use a resource tool to help us develop that habit. This is a tool to help you think things through and identify what to do next when you are planning a new change, or simply to be better at managing a change when one comes up.

Here, then, for you to use with any change you would like to manage successfully, is **Your Personal Book of Changes.**

MY
PERSONAL
BOOK OF CHANGES

NAME _____

DATE _____

I. IDENTIFYING THE CHANGE

A. *The change you are dealing with:* _____
_____

B. *This is a change of:*
Loss _____   Separation _____   Relocation _____
Relationship _____   Direction _____   Health _____
Personal Growth _____   Other _____

C. *Do you recognize and understand the change?* Yes _____
No _____

D. *Write a brief summary of the change, its effects, and what it could mean to you.* _____
_____
_____
_____

II. A PERSONAL QUESTIONNAIRE

1. *Is the change something that happened in the past, or is it happening now, in the present?* _____

2. *Is the change certain to happen, is it only "possible," or could it just be imagined?* _____

3. *Is this change temporary, or is it permanent?* _____

4. *Who or what is in control of the effects of this change now?*
_____

5. *Is there a way to minimize any negative effects of the change?*
_____
_____

6. *What do you stand to lose because of this change?*
_____

7. *What do you stand to gain from this change?*
_____

8. How can you maximize the "positive," or beneficial, effects of this change? _____

_____

9. What are the other changes that are brought on by this change?

_____

_____

10. Who else is affected by this change?

_____

11. What are the effects this change is having on you now?

_____

_____

12. If this change is causing a real problem, what is the real fear?

_____

13. How strongly is this change affected by the emotions involved? (Rate from 1 to 10, with 1 being not at all, and 10 being very strongly.)
   a. Your emotions _____
   b. Someone else's emotions _____

14. Is this a change that you wanted to happen? _____

15. What result do you want to avoid?

_____

_____

16. What result do you want to create?

_____

_____

17. Is this change significantly different from other major changes you have gone through—and if so, how is it different?

_____

18. What is one thing you could do right now to make dealing with this change work better for you?

_____

19. Regarding this change, whose opinions, including your own, are you listening to most?

_____

20. If you were asked to rate the level of self-confidence you have in dealing with this change (from 1 to 10), how would you rate yourself?
(1 is no confidence; 10 is high confidence) _____

21. In dealing with this change, what will the most likely outcome be if you take no action at all? _____
_____

22. What—if anything—is working against you in dealing with this change? _____

III. YOUR PERSONAL OBJECTIVES

A. What is the primary objective that you want to work on?
_____
_____

B. If you have a secondary objective, what is it?
_____
_____

C. If you have any other objectives or agendas for this change that you want to work on, what are they?
_____
_____

IV. PUTTING THE KEY VOCABULARY INTO PRACTICE

NOTE: After each of the following key words, write a one-line statement in first person ("I . . .") that accurately describes how you choose to see yourself dealing with this change. Some of the suggested phrases that appeared in Chapter 25 are included in this exercise as examples for you to follow.

1. Anticipate
(Example: "I anticipate, plan, and prepare. I am successful, and I am always ready, in the most positive possible way, for what lies ahead. I anticipate.")

_____

_____

2. Choice
(Example: "I make choices. I choose to choose in everything I do.")

_____

_____

3. Belief / Believe
(Example: "I believe in myself. With my strength, my confidence, and my belief, I make achievement a way of life!)

_____

_____

4. Creative / Creativity
(Example: "I am creative. I have a good mind, and I use it well.")

_____

_____

5. Perspective
(Example: "I choose to keep a healthy balance and a clear perspective in everything I do.")

_____

_____

6. Goal
(Example: "I set goals. I think them through, I write them down, I review them each day, and I work to make them happen.")

_____
_____

7. Action
(Example: "I take action. I know what to do, and I get things done.")

_____
_____

8. Achieve / Achievement
(Example: "I am an achiever. Achievement to me is a way of life.")

_____
_____

9. Adapt / Adaptive
(Example: "I adapt to any situation well, but always by my own choosing.")

_____
_____

10. Excel
(Example: "I choose to excel, in times of change and throughout my life.")

_____
_____

V. YOUR INVENTORY OF ASSETS

A. List your strongest assets (that you can use to help you deal with this change). If necessary, have a friend help you with this. List a minimum of ten:

1. _____
2. _____
3. _____

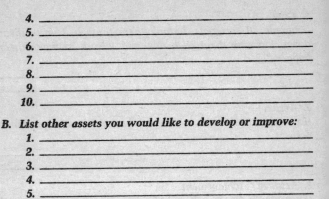

4. _____
5. _____
6. _____
7. _____
8. _____
9. _____
10. _____

B. **List other assets you would like to develop or improve:**
1. _____
2. _____
3. _____
4. _____
5. _____

VI. HOW YOU CHOOSE TO DEAL WITH THIS CHANGE

A. *Do you accept or reject the change?* Accept _____
Reject _____

B. *What are your reasons for accepting or rejecting the change?*
_____
_____
_____

C. *What ATTITUDE do you choose to have about this change?*
_____

D. *What STYLE do you choose to use in dealing with this change?*
1. *Acquiescence (giving in)* _____
2. *Partnership* _____
3. *Passive resistance* _____
4. *Active resistance* _____
5. *Full retreat* _____

6. *Active acceptance* _____
7. *Positive acceleration* _____

E. What principal form of ACTION do you choose to take in dealing with this change?

_____

_____

VII. YOUR PERSONAL ACTION PLAN

Today's date is: ___/___/___.

A. The first step I choose to take in dealing with this change is:

_____

_____

I will have completed my first action step by: ___/___/___.

B. The next action step I will take is:

_____

_____

I will begin this action step on: ___/___/___.
I will have completed this action step by: ___/___/___.

C. The third action step I will take in dealing with this change is:

_____

_____

I will begin this action step on: ___/___/___.
I will complete this action step by: ___/___/___.

D. What other action steps do you choose to take to deal with this change?

1. _____
   Action Date: ___/___/___
2. _____
   Action Date: ___/___/___
3. _____
   Action Date: ___/___/___

E. *Outline anything else that you would like to do, or feel you should do, that would help you deal with the change more effectively.*

_____
_____
_____
_____

VIII. OUTSIDE RESOURCES OR SUPPORT

List friends, associates, and organizations that you may want to call on for support or guidance in dealing with this change:

1. _____
2. _____
3. _____

   People who excel in a time of change are those who have practiced managing changes in a way that works. People who continue to struggle with change often spend as much (or more) energy fighting the changes or avoiding them, as they would dealing with them. People who deal with change well, *practice* doing it well.

27

The Ultimate Objective

Change has had too much control and too long a reign. It is time we took the control of change for ourselves. It has tried in every way to confuse us, overwhelm us, and confound us—and at times it has done a pretty good job of it.

But the people who successfully deal with change realize that it doesn't have to be a complicated matter at all. They have *simplified* the process of dealing with change. Instead of being confounded by the "turbulence" of change and worrying unnecessarily, they recognize the change, try to understand it, and take action to deal with it effectively.

The ultimate objective is to come out on top. It is to win and to manifest success through change instead of allowing change to manifest chaos in our lives. The problem is that we so often see change as *confronting* us as opposed to being a natural part of who we are and what our lives are all about.

It is apparent from even the briefest look at our own history that change itself is one of the most undeniable and predictable aspects of our lives. The truth is, change in any of its forms should never be allowed to surprise us or confuse us. If we are intelligent, we ought to expect change, anticipate it and beat it at its own game.

It is time we learned. Change is not the enemy—change is much more the town crier, the boy who runs across the cobblestone streets at night, shouting out the news of the events in our lives that affect all of us. We have learned that we cannot sleep through the news; it is better to be *aware*.

So it is strange that so many people go through their lives stating that there is too much change. That is like saying there is too much sky or too much earth, or too much *life* to deal with. Meanwhile, there are those few among us who have learned to see the changes in life as a *part* of life. They are the most alive, and they are the ones who win the most.

The objective of any good learning program is not just to impart information; it is to help the individual apply what he or she has learned. If you now were to do nothing more than to use this book as a refresher course, reread the personal exercises and complete **Your Personal Book of Changes** even once or twice a year, the positive results you achieve for yourself could create lasting benefits in your life.

But the ultimate objective is most certainly not only to do well in dealing with change. The ultimate objective must clearly be to rise above ourselves and to excel with change *in spite of* change and *because of* change. Understanding *that* is understanding the basic structure of our involvement with life as individuals. Without change we are nothing. *With* change we have the chance to be everything that we could dream of being.

■ *Learning to Grow*

In closing this book on the process of dealing with change more effectively, I will relate to you one final story. If makes the point better than any other way I could say it.

I grew up in a small town in the middle of the farmlands in a midwestern state. In those days I often made money—and not very much at that—pulling, by hand, the weeds and the sunflowers and the sharp, cutting thistles from the rows of soybeans that the farmers raised in the surrounding area. It was enough to keep me in blue jeans and shoes and gave me a little pocket money to now and then buy a book or to see a movie.

When I was working in the fields, I knew two farmers—I'll call them Farmer Brown and Farmer Jones. Their farms were adjacent to each other, and equal in size—each about six or seven hundred acres of farmland—and each of the two farmers raised the same crops. The similarities between their farms, being next to each other, were such that there was almost no discernible difference between them. The only thing that separated the farms was an old barbed-wire fence that marked a boundary line between one farmer's land and the other's. Everything else was the same. They received the same rain, the same dry spells, the same late summer hailstorms, and the same late dry autumns of the year in which to harvest their crops.

The farmer who I am calling Farmer Jones was one of the happiest men that I had ever met. I don't know what it was about him that made him seem so full of life, but he had an attitude that I never forgot. His neighbor, Farmer Brown, had an entirely different attitude about life. Farmer Jones seemed to see a hailstorm as a momentary quirk of nature and something that he could live through, while Farmer Brown saw the same hailstorm not only as something that could ruin his crops, but as a reinforcement to his own self-doubt that he could ever succeed.

I was sixteen years old when the winds came, and they brought with them incessant rain and, eventually, pounding hail. Ice balls the size of marbles, and then golf balls, plummeted down from the heavens and smashed themselves into the fields, leveling the ground of the farmlands into useless and worthless pulp. All the farms suffered, and the crops and the farmlands of Farmer Jones and Farmer Brown suffered equal damage.

Farmer Jones took these things in stride. But Farmer Brown was different. Farmer Brown was a complainer; he complained about everything. In five minutes Farmer Brown could find more fault with anything and everything than most of the other farmers could find in a week.

The next year Farmer Jones planted his crops again. He planted more corn that he had ever planted before; he planted wheat and soybeans and flax, and he fully expected his crops to grow and to flourish and at harvest to bring a good market price.

Meanwhile, Farmer Brown, who lived next door— only a half a mile down the road from Farmer Jones— had all but given up. The rows of corn that he had planted in the spring were filled with weeds and grasses that would bleed the energy and the vitality from the stalks of corn, causing them to wither and fail. Farmer Brown's wheat crop that year was a feeble attempt at growing wheat, and within a few weeks of the planting, the field was overgrown with weeds.

And Farmer Brown should never have planted his soybeans at all. Believing that his crop would never mature to a plentiful harvest, Farmer Brown had given up. Where there should have been a strong and invigorated field of soybeans, there stood instead a promising patch of thistles, almost overshadowed by the broad leaves of crop-destroying wild sunflowers.

I was young at the time, but I was old enough to learn a lesson that I have never forgotten. Farmer Jones and Farmer Brown lived on the same land, with the same opportunity. To most observers, it was the simple change of a summer storm that separated one from the other. But to my mind, I saw a greater difference between the two of them.

Farmer Jones had a different attitude about change—a different approach to life. He had a goal—a longer-term objective—that he saw in front of him. Farmer Brown, his closest neighbor, suffering the same defeat and having the same potential, chose to fail instead of succeed.

Farmer Brown, lacking the initiative and the understanding to deal with change in a positive way, had failed. Farmer Jones, who had dealt with the same circumstances in his life in a different way, had chosen to succeed in spite of it all. One of them let his crops fail and go to waste; the other planted new seeds and moved on.

No one I know who likes himself at all wants to be a Farmer Brown and let those valuable crops of life go to waste. Most of us would prefer to be a Farmer Jones. We would like to make things grow.

The life you have in front of you may not be as simple as planting crops, working the fields, and seeing them come to fruition. But then, if you think about it, that is what most of us do. We may think we are doing exceptionally important things—meeting deadlines, making life work, and moving on from where we are now to where we are going. But when it all comes down to it, I suspect that what we are really doing is trying to plant an acre or two and trying to make it grow.

Then along comes change that interrupts the growing process. Some of us will find within the change a reason to stop, and to become less than that which we should have been. Others among us will find a reason to grow and to become better than we thought we could have been.

The final objective is to grow.

And the only true opportunity anyone has ever found to grow is with *change*. In your time of change, I trust you will choose to excel. I know you have chosen to grow.